"*Restoring Venus* is a brave, heart-breaking, heart-warming story of an amazing woman's journey through life with pain. Amy's story is told honestly, without bitterness, though it may be hard for some healthcare providers to hear that our words sometimes harm and limit the very people we are trying to help. Humans are strong and resilient, and Amy is proof of that. This is a story that will give hope to those in pain."

—Sarah Haag, PT, DPT

"This inspiring book brings amazing insights into how someone in pain lives, makes decisions and how they interpret the information healthcare providers give them. It felt like I had crawled inside her thoughts. This book is a must read for anyone in pain or helping people in pain."

—Antony Lo, *The Physio Detective,*
*APA Musculoskeletal Physiotherapist,*
*Associate of the Australian College of Physiotherapists*

"This is awesome! Amy Eicher's writing style is expressive, easy to follow and enlightening. Her description of the first few post-operative days is powerful. By baring her soul, we learn how a person in pain thinks and how her beliefs drive actions through a long journey that finally leads to health.

—Mark Kargela, *PT, DPT, OCS, cert-MDT, MTC,*
*FAAOMPT Founder of Modern Pain Care*

"Amy Eicher's skill in weaving together this incredible story of pain, hope, and survival is a must-read for medical practitioners who work with pain patients. *Restoring Venus* provides insight and will be a helpful resource for caretakers of family members living with pain, as well as provide comfort for those who are currently living with persistent pain and who may feel alone and unheard."
—Rajam Roose, *LMT, Founder of San Diego Pain Summit, author of* Travels With A Road Dog: Hitchhiking Along the Roads of the Americas

"The raw emotion, honesty, and in-depth self-reflection expressed in this book are powerful and moving. Having worked with thousands of people in pain, I can say with unwavering confidence that the detailed look into the private life, thoughts, fears, emotions, and struggles of someone living with chronic pain is among the most valuable resources any healthcare provider who works with those in pain could have. Amy Eicher makes clear that understanding the person behind the pain … is the future of pain care."
—Jarod Hall, *PT, DPT, OCS, CSCS*

"The raw honesty of the challenges and triumphs of Amy Eicher's journey through pain and back is impressive. This book shines a light through the conflicting information encountered along the way, and the importance of being true to yourself."
—Sandy Hilton, *PT, DPT, MS*

# Restoring Venus

A Journey from Chronic Pain to Possibilities

Amy Eicher

Restoring Venus
Copyright © 2019 by Amy Eicher

No part of this book may be reproduced without written permission from the publisher or copyright holders, except for a reviewer who may quote brief passages in a review; nor may any part of this book be reproduced, stored in a retrieval system, or transmitted in any form or by any means (electronic, mechanical, photocopying, recording or other) without written permission from the publisher or copyright holders.

Printed by B.C. Allen Publishing and Tonic Books

144 N 7th St. #525
Brooklyn, NY 11249


Now taking manuscript submissions and book ideas at any stage of the process:
submissions@tonicbooks.online

Printed in the United States of America

Photographer: Robin Nordmeyer
Cover Design: Maria Alcoke
Interior Design: Susan Veach

ISBN: 978-0-9980299-1-7

# Why Restoring Venus

A long time ago, while I was in physical therapy for the billionth time, things were finally starting to change. My PT looked at me and asked if I knew who the Venus de Milo was.

My response: "The statue of the chick with no arms?"

He sighed, looked at me, and said, "Yes, Amy, the chick with no arms. You are like her."

The Venus de Milo, also known as the Aphrodite of Melos, was created a long time ago. It is one of the most famous works of ancient Greek sculpture. This statue depicts the goddess of love and beauty, Aphrodite, also known as Venus. The craftsmanship is amazing, its worth is priceless, and it is displayed at the Louvre art museum in France.

Before being displayed in one of the most famous art museums in the world, however, it was found in 1820, in the ancient city of Melos—buried under the rubble, hidden away, no longer able to be enjoyed, and forgotten about. This beautiful statue must have been a wreck when it was found. Can you imagine the layers of dirt and grime that covered this masterpiece? It had been buried there for many hundreds of years.

I felt a lot like that description when I was in the midst of my pain. Lost. Hidden away. Broken.

For me, this statue resonates with my heart. Something that was once vibrant and a centerpiece of activity had been hidden away and broken, seemingly forgotten about, until the day it was accidentally found. It was not in the same shape it had been, but now it was something much more.

We are all masterpieces waiting to be found and restored. There are still so many reasons to hope, no matter where you are in your journey with pain. You are not alone, and you have so much to give. You—yes, you—*you* have so much to give and share with the world, and I hope you are encouraged to restore your hope and yourself. This is my story of my restoration.

Amy

Swimming without Arms

In a Georgia hospital room, waiting for a surgery I wasn't sure I needed, I startled every time I heard footfalls squeak loudly in the hallway.

"Ben, is that them?"

"I don't know."

"I wish they'd come for me!"

We held our collective breath, wondering if the curtain in my segment of the pre-op room would push open and we'd see a nurse's smiling face. We'd been waiting for nearly an hour, and my lower body was stained from the weird brownish orange of Betadine.

When the footfalls passed and faded into the distance, Ben relaxed. But not me. Relax? My heart pounded like thunder. It reminded me that I was not the Venus de Milo, an iconic work of art pulled from ruins and revered forevermore. I was a broken American wife and mother who had been buried in crippling pain and anguish for eighteen fucking years. The long journey had isolated me from family and friends—society, shopping malls, church, swim meets—and today marked my last best hope to finally be fixed, by a surgeon who would implant five screws into my pelvis. Sound like fun?

Or he would fail, like all the other diggers and excavators of misery had failed me in years past. And that's why I could not quiet my head and heart.

*I cannot live this way anymore!*

The many medical institutions I'd visited through the years all seemed the same: the sterile glow of humming florescent lights; the plastic-covered mattress that crinkled noisily every time I adjusted my body, which I did often thanks to the itchy and threadbare bluish gown that tormented me (the tie strings were torn, the hem and seams were shabby, and the opening in the rear refused to fully cover my backside). And it all made me wonder: if surgical procedures were extremely expensive technological wonders, why couldn't these health emporiums figure out how to design a decent garment for ailing people, who already feel vulnerable?

More footsteps. I grabbed the ice-cold metal bars on each side of the bed and then rejected them. Ben was in the chair next to my bed, but I felt very alone.

"Good morning."

The anesthesiologist was tall and smiling. Despite his friendly bedside manner, I found it difficult to smile back. "So can you knock me out now?"

"Ah no. We have to wait for your physical therapist. She doesn't like it when I knock out a patient before she has had her visit."

What was keeping her? She would align me in the operating room before the orthopedic surgeon could do his thing. I wanted to get this show on the road. "Will she be here soon?" I asked.

"I think so." Another smile, and he was gone.

When the door closed, a panic attack began. My mind burned with one ugly truth: this surgery was a horrible mistake.

*Get me out of here!*

Tunnel vision blinded me. I was completely unaware of Ben or anything else in my little area. All I heard were the voices of doctors, one after another, pounding me with opinions, groupthink, suspicions.

"There is no reason a woman your age should be in this much pain!"

"You are too young for this barbaric surgery!"

"If it goes wrong, no one can help you afterward!"

The next wave of pompous doctors was even louder. If only I could swim away, beneath the surface, where it would be quiet. But my arms fell away; my legs wouldn't kick.

"You just need to try harder."

"Have you really explored every option?"

"Maybe you like living this way!"

*This is not living!*

"Maybe you just want the prescription drugs."

*I'm not an addict; I'm in pain.*

"We can't find a problem."

"You must be depressed."

"It's all in your head."

*No, my pelvis is twisted out of place.*

I heard a symphony of physical therapists, chiropractors, and one doctor of osteopathy telling me I had to be aligned or the surgery would fail and I'd be even more crippled.

As the voices kept crashing, I wondered, *Where is my physical therapist! Position my body*—please—*so they can shoot me up and put me under.*

Swimming had once been my refuge. My body, an arrow effortlessly gliding through water, had been confirmation. I had been gifted, successful, in control. I had won competitions; I had been scouted, praised; and I had then been awarded an NCAA swimming scholarship, only to have had it ripped to shreds months later after one painful flip turn in the pool. Something in my body had snapped. But it could have been an avalanche for all the ways it had altered my life. It had broken me in half.

I was the Venus de Milo. But unlike the fractured masterpiece discovered on an Aegean island, I would probably never be revered for my flaws and inherent beauty. Had God punished me for my sins? *I know I'm damaged goods, but dear God, fix me. Or bring me someone who can. An explorer with a sixth sense. Let him dig me out of the ruins of my life. When his shovel clanks against something hard, let him drop to his knees and frantically push away the last layer of soil to behold my nude torso. Lost and now found!*

I heard Ben say, "Becky!"

My physical therapist arrived as my emotional dam broke. Hysterical tears and anxiety poured out of me. She rushed forward.

"Amy, what?"

In a panic, I pleaded, "This has to work!"

"It will, Amy; you will have your life back."

Her hand rubbed my arm. It was comforting to be touched, a soothing balm. Between crying fits, I spit out the words again: "This—has—to—work."

She repeated, with utter confidence, "It will."

As she made a show of looking at my pelvic landmarks and adjusting my position, I surrendered to the moment. The crying stopped, and I told myself that I needed to be strong for Ben and the kids.

Oozing Southern charm, Becky assured me, "Everything is just right." I wondered if that was the same line she used for all the other desperate housewives with sacroiliac joint dysfunction. "Remember, I'll be there with you in the operating room. Once we're inside, I'll adjust your pelvis again, OK?"

"Whatever. Just knock me out. *Please.*"

As if by command, the smiley anesthesiologist was back.

*Ah, drugs!*

My mind began to swim away as a cold substance delivered through the IV snaked into my bloodstream.

I turned and realized a blurry version of Ben was standing there, holding a bulging clear bag that contained my clothes and other belongings. My dopey brain pondered, Why can't they make those bags big enough for my stuff?

My mouth formed words that sounded fuzzy and well-worn. I was trying to be strong because I was afraid Ben couldn't handle any more of my fragile-wife routine.

"Ben, I'll be OK. I'll make this work, OK?"

"I know you will. Don't worry about me."

"I won't let you down anymore. I-I-I...won't..."

That last word came out in a whisper as the gurney began to sail. All I could see in the hallway were dotted white ceiling tiles with alternating patterns that shimmered in gaudy fluorescent light.

A blast of cold made me shiver as we rolled through slim silver doors into the operating arena. A huge purplish beam illuminated the middle of the room, which was surrounded by an army of doctors and nurses wearing blue scrubs. Was I hallucinating? Each appeared ready for excavation, armed with a shovel, pick, or ax.

On the verge of blacking out—my prayers finally being answered—a face appeared. I felt my lips spread into a soft, messy smile as the figure spoke. A mask muffled the words, so I couldn't tell if this person was wishing me well or was actually saying, "We have come to dig you out of ancient ruins and restore you. Are you ready to live again, Venus?"

*Will I have arms?*

# Part One

Although my burial did not last quite as long as the Venus de Milo's, my disappearance from family and social life felt like an eternal curse.

# Chapter 1

The effects of the medication dampened my senses and, thankfully, dulled my frayed emotions. There was still snow on the ground from the freak storm three days before. I'd been angry about the delay it caused, but now the white stuff was comforting because it reflected shafts of blinding southern sunshine through the window in my hospital room.

I was out of surgery, awake, and alive, with a burning need to call Mom and Dad; my best friend, Jess; and a physical therapist named Tim, whose gallant but failed attempt to restore my damaged body and soul had led me to the operating room. I wanted them all to know that I hadn't died under the knife or been paralyzed from the waist down with a bent screw jammed into a spinal nerve.

Earlier in the week, I had made my husband, Ben, promise to take charge once I was out of surgery.

"Dear, if you love me at all, you will not let me use the phone while I am high on drugs."

"Yeah, OK."

"No. Not 'OK.' Promise. *Please*. No matter how much I beg and plead, *do not let me have the phone*. You make the calls."

"Sure. Of course."

"No. Not 'of course.' You tell them I'm, you know—tell them whatever condition I'm in. I don't need stories floating around on Facebook about how I sang some silly song or said something amazingly stupid, like pledging my undying love and devotion to the orderly or shift nurse."

"Yeah, yeah, yeah."

"No. Don't say—"

"Hey." Ben shut me up, then put his arms around me for comfort. "I'd never let you hurt yourself."

"Promise?"

My pained, desperate expression made him smile. "OK, Amy, I promise I will not let you have your cell phone, no matter who you want to call or how awful you're being to me."

"'Awful'? What do you mean—?"

"You have my word."

A kiss on the forehead ended that talk. My Ben. A good man. When I couldn't take care of the kids, he was there: steady while I wobbled up and down stairs or felt like I might collapse waiting in the grocery store line.

It was a smart move to put him in charge because after the operation I was drugged up for sure. Oral meds blended with intravenous injections and drips, and I wasn't shy about asking for more when the pain ebbed, then rushed back in. Feel No Pain was my motto. *Got drugs? I'll take those now.* I was done with feeling all that pain.

As my head cleared, I could assess my body and overall condition. I realized my breathing was shallow, and I was stiff, like I'd been frozen in a butcher's meat locker. I was unwilling to attempt movement. Just the thought choked me with fear.

*What if I move, and it really hurts?*

*What if the surgery failed?*

One litany after another messed with my head, despite the drugs and purple haze they caused.

*What if the pain never leaves?*

*What if I still can't bear weight?*

*What if we did all this and not a fucking thing changes?*

An all-too-familiar tightness in my chest threatened to pull me into a kind of post-traumatic stress episode. I fought it. *No. I'm not letting myself go there again.* I couldn't let myself be drowned by an emotional torrent of a past littered with failed treatments, false hopes, and despair.

My mental anguish was arrested by my husband's warm voice. "You're awake? How do you feel?"

"I…don't know yet? I am afraid to find out," I whispered, in a raspy voice that didn't sound like my own. That's when I remembered a tube had been inserted in my mouth and pushed down my throat.

A glass of water appeared. Ben encouraged me to drink. "Take a moment and figure it out, then let me know."

Soon I discovered that both butt cheeks were very painful. Everything felt swollen, and it hurt to move. I had been told the postoperative pain wouldn't be too bad. I wondered if maybe something was wrong because this didn't feel good. There was tremendous pain when I attempted to move my body and engage the muscle that had just been invaded by my surgeon. My instinct was to stay still and breathe until the post-op pain went away.

But what should I say to my husband to assure him? What should I tell this man who had mostly stood by me and cared for me and honored our marital vows, in sickness and in health? Illness is destructive not only to the body. It also messes with the mind; the tightening twist of guilt and shame can be every bit as damaging. I'd been through hell and back several times. I wanted him to know I could get through this and get my life back.

"I'm really sore and afraid to move—I don't want to screw up the surgery."

"You can't move the screws, Amy; they're in there good and tight."

"I think I should stay here in bed, just be motionless, until the pain goes away."

My well-made plan was soon scuffled by nature's call: I needed to use the bathroom, but the idea of standing up was terrifying. The machines and monitors, with all their colors, noises, and connective cables, made me realize that getting to the toilet would have been difficult even for an agile person. But I was not going to use a bedpan. Nope. My last sliver of dignity would not allow that.

The first attempt to get out of bed made my body groan in protest. Thanks a lot, girl. Just had my butt cut into and now this! Can't I just rest a little longer? When

I was on my feet, my legs felt like Jell-O. I was a newborn colt. Or Bambi in the Disney movie where Thumper observes the fawn's first steps and says, "Kind of wobbly, aren't ya!"

I shuffled more than walked. Yet being able to move at all was encouraging. I made it to the bedside commode—surprise!—did my business, then made it back to bed, where I planned to spend the rest of the day sleeping. As I lay down and relaxed, I imagined myself in a swimming pool, floating…

## NATURAL AFFINITY

Swimming, or just being near water, always appealed to me. As a child, I excelled in swim classes, where I felt at home submerged or effortlessly gliding in a pool from one end to the other. On vacations, at motels, my dad and I would race laps, and all summer long I was happy to hang around an outdoor pool from sunup to sundown. Although friends had asked me to join the summer swim teams, I was always out of town when tryouts were scheduled.

The summer of 1987, after seventh grade, I was home and finally tried out. I was so nervous that I flailed and swallowed gulps of water, more a drowning victim than a wannabe Olympic athlete. But thankfully swimming isn't exactly a sport that cuts players from the team. I persevered and eventually won races.

Early-morning practices consumed me, and though freestyle was my first love, I was determined to learn all the strokes. I progressed quickly, and my confidence soared. Finally, I was good at something.

By my second meet, I'd shaken off my nerves, my efficiency and speed had improved, and I won my first-ever ribbon. Proud of myself? You bet I was. I liked being a winner after struggling academically in school, failing at all sports that required a ball, achieving mediocrity in ballet class (I'd change from swimsuit to leotard in Mom's car). It had been hard not knowing how to manage my awkward, lanky body. For years I had felt like a puppy skidding on a slippery floor with impossibly gigantic feet.

But in the water, that all changed. I was a dolphin. Awkward and clumsy? Not anymore. The pool transformed me. Now I was long, strong, and beautiful. I was home.

In the eighth grade, my first full season, I flourished and qualified for the state championship meet on a relay. That was a big deal. I felt special and honored to be the fourth swimmer, and I wanted badly to do well for the other three girls on my team. While my coaches were encouraging, no one on the outside made much of it. Yet inside I was growing in leaps and bounds. I had figured out what it meant to work hard and savored the positive outcomes. Self-reliance bloomed as I pushed harder than I ever thought possible. Dreams were born and fulfilled.

The fall of 1988, I was one of five freshmen swimmers chosen to be on the varsity squad. I was dumbstruck. Swimming competitively with seniors? Learning to chase faster girls only made *me* faster. I was all ears when my coaches spoke about improving my technique in the pool. I was gung ho about seeing what my body and spirit were truly capable of.

At that time, I also got my first job, giving swimming lessons at the YMCA and coaching the eight-and-under kids. I loved working with the itty-bitty swimmers. It was so much fun watching them launch from the starting blocks and chase their dreams.

In my sophomore year, I again reached a lofty goal: qualifying for the high school state meet, in an individual event. I qualified in the one-hundred-yard freestyle by the skin of my teeth—not a nanosecond to spare. These days 55.10 seconds doesn't sound so fast, but my coaches talked effusively about believing I was capable of being one of the first women to break 50 seconds. I thought they were crazy or just trying to give me confidence. In a world where time is measured in hundredths of seconds, how the heck could I be proclaimed Most Likely to Succeed? Could a woman, any woman, really go that fast?

Years later I would understand why my coaches were ecstatic. I had dropped five seconds off my time in one year and was growing, gaining muscle, and developing quickly into an elite swimmer. That summer I went to the US YMCA national championships in Orlando, Florida, with just my parents and a coach from another swim club. Our local YMCA hadn't seen the need to send a coach for one swimmer. I swam in the same event (not the same heat) as Janet Evans, who had already won three gold medals in the 1988 Seoul Olympics and held multiple world records in distance events. I was in awe of her and my own accomplishment.

As I progressed through high school, I realized my athleticism was not only about me and the coordination of my body and mind. When you begin to succeed, others see you differently. In one way or another, you're asked to carry the weight of leadership. The responsibilities grew with my personal best in competition, and I was always chasing a new goal or a better swimmer. I'd even try to pass the slower swimmers in practice for a second time if it meant I might achieve the impossible.

Pushing my limits—with hunger and devotion.

Technique and training—with precision and passion.

I loved pouring all of myself into workouts: pushing my limits and seeing what happened; playing with the pitch of my hand to see if it would make me that much faster; pushing past what I felt were my limits to find new ones. Every challenge was exhilarating to me.

Recruiting letters from large and small universities began to arrive. I was making waves in the right kind of way, all the while trying to be a team player and set a good example to the underclassmen about setting goals and working hard to reach them.

Yet something else was happening beneath the surface. Sensations. And the sensations weren't all pure. I was a seventeen-year-old girl whose hormones had begun to race. I felt conflicted about certain urges. I'd been going to Young Life—a Christian ministry—for a while and was very involved. I loved Bible study and the philosophical discussions they inspired. At the same time, slowly, I was being lured toward my sexual initiation.

By an older man.

By an older *married* man.

By an older married *Christian* man.

To everyone else, Jeff was a mentor and unwavering cheerleader. His encouragement was a bottomless resource. He taught me about Jesus and God's never-ending love for all of humanity…and for me, a gutsy athlete who had traded ballet slippers for a Speedo. An innocent with a ripe body and a pliable, eager mind who had never been wooed or known such charm and full-on male attention. Attention that seemed wholesome. How could it be anything else? We were Christians, and I was a virgin.

Then one day everything changed: we became lovers, and demons began to taunt me even as I relished the erotic pleasures of coupling and multiple orgasms. I was no longer a woman gliding like an arrow through a lap pool. Sex was a sensuous stream that swam through my core, enlivening every nerve, leaving me limp with a satisfaction I'd never known. The pool had taught me to compete. In my newfound expression of sexuality, I found the will to surrender.

But I could not share my excitement with anyone but Jeff. My teammates couldn't know. My parents? Really? How about my friends in Young Life? No way. Good Christian girls shouldn't like sex or want it. No one would ever understand. I'd be labeled a slut or a whore.

## DAY TWO POST-OP

Between all the poking, prodding, and monitoring any reasonable person would expect in a hospital, during my two nights there, I was also awash in pain meds, rotating nurse visits, blood pressure tests, meals, and drugged sleep. But at least I no longer suffered the unfashionable and continuously scratchy and annoying hospital gown.

Before Ben and I had traveled to Georgia for the procedure, our kids had shopped with me to choose cute and stylish PJs. The soft fabric comforted me and brought me closer to my babies, even while I moaned and groaned in my bed. The garments also reminded me that Connor and Erin were safe in Illinois with their loving grandma, my mother-in-law. I was free to be miserable as I literally took my first steps toward recovery.

"Ready to get up and go?"

The hospital physical therapist had arrived cheery, with the intention of helping me walk the hallways of the hospital. She maneuvered a walker close to my bed for support. This brought my mom to mind. So many times in the past, I had been the concerned daughter watching her lean against a walker while healing after one too many hospital stays. Now it was my turn. But the walker was only one new reality I had to accept.

The therapist held out the gait belt.

"Oh, please," I said.

The thickly woven cotton belt with pastel stripes helped caregivers keep a grip in case a patient lost his or her balance. But it bugged me. Something about it was humiliating. For years I'd dragged myself around my home and my town and somehow boarded a plane to Georgia. I didn't like being forced now to wear what amounted to a dog leash. The indignity.

*I don't need that. I can walk. Wasn't your surgery supposed to fix my pelvis, screw it in place? That damned thing is used for old people.* I DON'T NEED IT!

The rage stayed in my head, but I wanted to scream. "Do I have to?"

"Yes, it's the rules. I just want you to be safe."

Oh, how I wanted to prove to myself and everyone else that I could leap out of this bed and walk down the hall like anyone else in that building.

But that wasn't going to happen. My anger subsided as I sat up and the PT secured the belt snuggly around my waist. When I put my hands on the walker, she cooed, "Ready to stand?"

I took a deep breath, cleared my mind, and rose to my feet. An involuntary smile spread across my face; my eyes opened wide. Oh my, I thought, *this is different.* This is what standing is supposed to feel like—sound balance, sturdy, secure! The usual sensation, the one that felt like my entire right hip might collapse and sink into my body, was gone. I was no longer unstable. I think I really exhaled for the first time in years.

Also, the fire ants that for years had taken up residence throughout my entire backside, from my hamstrings down low and up through my buttocks, were no longer biting at me, causing a constant blazing pain. Was it the medication that made this first walking attempt so sweet, or was the ordeal of suffering for eighteen years really gone? Then it hit me: in the past no medication had successfully relieved that pain. A gush of hope caught my heart by surprise.

I scuffled to the doorway and peered around the corner to get a look at the long corridor. I wondered how far this PT would want me to walk. She didn't instill the confidence that Tim, my PT at home, did. But I could hear him chide me and remind me to behave. I had no idea how far I'd last. Not so far, I feared, despite my determination. Could the Venus de Milo have answered the call after she had been restored?

I looked at my gait-belt master, speechless.

"Let's see if you can make it to that picture there." She pointed to a painting within a stone's throw of my door.

"I'd rather swim it, if you don't mind."

I laughed at her expression. She had no idea that I had once been a star athlete who for a time had floated through life's challenges with the ease of an eel. "Sorry. Of course I can walk to that picture."

*Steady as she goes, Amy. You can do whatever you set your mind to; you always have, especially with the right coach by your side.* This young woman would have to do. I would comply even though I feared my legs might not cooperate. The PT walked behind me, firm grip on leash.

Step one. Not quite like walking on water. I felt like a tugboat navigating the wide berth of the oceanic hallway.

Step two. My legs were cumbersome under me. I didn't walk so much as shuffle.

Somehow my vessel, this creaky body, reached the framed picture, and I was relieved—until I turned around and looked back at the length I'd traveled. My room was a distant horizon, and my steps had been tentative, uncontrolled, unsure. Then my legs began to whimper.

"I think this is as far as I can go."

The confession made me blush. I was pleading for mercy. Where was the swimming champ now, after only forty feet of walking? She was exhausted and ready to call it quits. No Olympic medal for me.

You could have mopped the floor with the tears I rained. With gritted teeth, I raised my imaginary sail, hoping a light breeze might assist me. But it never came. I was stuck there, in the middle of a vast sea otherwise known as a hospital corridor. The only way back was…

Step one.

Step two.

The physical therapist removed the gait belt as soon as I reached my bed. As I lay back and closed my eyes, I smiled. A smile for me only. For the first time in many, many long miserable years, I felt…I felt solid, stable, like my body was, once again, all one piece. Like…

I was asleep before my busy mind could prepare me for the challenges to come: *Many rivers to cross, girl. Venus wasn't rebuilt in a day.*

# Chapter 2

By the time I was released from the hospital, I was starting to move my body a bit without fear of coming apart at the seams. Moving wasn't easy, and it took a lot of willpower to believe I could do it. But by the time Ben and I checked into the very nice hotel across the street, I was waking up to the idea of trying to be normal, despite all the energy it required.

Our room was a reprieve from the medical environment. Hey, it would have been romantic, if not for my compromised body and my very real concerns about hopping on a plane home the next day. Forget about the flight back to Normal—a city name that continued to reverberate with irony. How was I going to survive the hour-long car ride to the airport and then the pomp and circumstance of passing through security to get to our gate?

Then I thought of Venus and could not remember how long she had been buried underground. Probably longer than a half day of discomfort. But I was not made of marble. And she was not made of flesh and blood. And not to pry, but had she ever won a swimming event or cried when the victories stopped and the misery began?

During the postoperative checkup with my surgeon, I had learned that he had inserted a third screw on my left side to make sure he had achieved "purchase" in my pelvic bones. He had seemed so pleased. "Nice," I had said, which had been followed by my blank smile.

Later, alone with Ben, I had asked, "Why do they bother telling patients anything in the hospital? It's not like we remember any of it."

"It *happened*. That's all you need to know," he had said.

He had been right. That extra screw would certainly explain, in my mind, why my left side hurt so much more than the right.

So my surgeon had signed my release, and even Becky, the physical therapist that had adjusted my pelvis prior to surgery, had paid a visit to check my pelvic alignment. I had officially had her approval that my alignment was "perfect" and my instability was gone.

In the hotel, Ben woke me so that we could get ready to head to the airport, and he'd brought food from the breakfast buffet. I had other plans. For the several years I had been eating meals in my bed alone, I was hungry for company.

"Let's have breakfast together. At a table. With other human beings. I'm a *people* person."

"Are you sure?" he asked.

"That I'm a people person?"

"I know you're a people person—I know that. I mean the sitting."

"It will show me I can survive the flight home."

I knew I needed to walk and sit because I'd spent the last three days lying down 99.5 percent of the time. Walking and sitting were hard work. That's why I'd avoided them.

Ben grabbed my walker and helped me to my feet. He held the door as I entered the hallway. It was long. They all are when your butt burns with pain. But I felt ready to tackle this hallway, even though my trek to the dining room would be the farthest I had yet walked.

By the time we reached the front desk, my knuckles had turned white because I was leaning as much of my weight as possible onto my hands. Think about it. Our feet and legs were designed to bear the weight of our bodies. Now most of that poundage was the responsibility of eight fingers, two thumbs, and a couple of sweaty palms. I could hear those extremities whine, *This is not fair!*

I didn't care about fair. At this point, I was concerned that the more my hands hurt, the longer the space between the continental breakfast buffet and I seemed to be. I was sure the distance kept elongating, distorting the way a fun house mirror stretches shapes and perceptions. Or like swimming in a lake to catch a lost beach ball that remains furiously out of reach no matter how fast you stroke the water.

I looked over my shoulder to measure how far the door to our room was: equidistant. I was stuck midway, between a firm bed and food. My longtime traveling companion—panic—was rumbling, ready to remind me that this was going all wrong. *Well that was dumb. Walk all the way to the buffet? Good luck, honey!*

*Shut up.* That's what I was thinking. Guilt and shame would show up next. No. That was not going to happen. DOWN! I barked in my head. I CAN DO THIS! Defiant and determined or just plain stubborn and stupid? Take your pick. But I shuffled on.

Once I reached the beverage service, I managed to pour a glass of orange juice for myself. Then I realized I had no way to carry it back to the table while holding onto the walker.

My shoulders slumped; my last breath gushed out of my lungs as tears crept into the corners of my eyes. It was only breakfast, but it was a bridge too far.

As panic, guilt, and shame converged for the kill, I felt Ben's arm around my waist. "Let me escort you to your table."

As I sat and drank my orange juice, I imagined the Venus de Milo sharing the meal with us. I doubt she would have complained if someone had spoon-fed her. So why should I? With Ben at my side, breakfast hit the spot. My frustrations dissolved. We ate well and then prepared for our flight home.

## SENIORITIS AND SEXUALITY

In high school, I was several months into what I thought was a torrid affair with my Young Life leader, yet despite the discovery of physical pleasure, the sexual relationship made me feel like a fraud. I assumed that everything that didn't go my way—not being elected captain, losing a race, catching the common cold—was either God's punishment or his protection. I fluctuated wildly between those two extremes. I may have been a committed young Christian, but I was not pure as the driven snow.

Regardless, excitement and a bit of pressure arrived as I was being recruited by college swim coaches, including Steve Paska, of Illinois State University, where I hoped to earn a teaching degree. Seemed like a good deal: get paid to swim for a college where I likely would have enrolled anyway. I signed on early and was set to start college as a Redbird.

My senior year also coincided with my high school coach's decision to retire. He was determined to win one last conference championship, so he worked us hard with no concern for the bigger picture. During an amazing conference meet, I won all four of my events, and our relay set a school record.

Yet by the time we arrived for the state meet, we were at the end of our taper, meaning we had slowly been backing off on training to build energy for the meet. To ensure a conference win with fast swims, our coach had started our taper early. There was no way we could keep up the pace for state competition. I placed thirteenth in both my individuals and the two relays I was part of. It was truly heartbreaking. I had placed first in all the same events at sectionals that year and was seeded in the top six in the state. All that work throughout the season with a coach who, in the end, only wanted one more feather in *his* cap. His last hurrah. But what about us? We were a talented team with goals of our own, but we were worn out by the coach's demands by the end of the season.

Punishment or protection?

That summer, like the previous one, I would be a nanny for the daughter of my high school athletic director, and I decided to take a few weeks off swimming. I'd been swimming for five years with barely a two-week break. It was time for some *me* time. As my high school career was ending, and a new phase of swim mania was about to begin, I had been determined to enjoy myself before the fall semester at ISU, and I had been given a key to Jeff's apartment.

## SUMMER OF 1991

For two years, Jeff had been grooming me for sexual abuse. He had been tutoring me in math, and one summer day before my senior year, as I did my homework, he turned me away from my studies and kissed me on the lips. The physical sensation was soft, warm, pleasant—and jarring, confusing and unexpected. I slapped him. Hard.

Why would he do this? He was a father figure to me. He quickly apologized, always the actor, and told me I was so beautiful he couldn't help himself. A married man, nine years older than me. He couldn't control himself? The kiss didn't feel like the affection of a parent—my own dad, for instance. Yet…

Throughout the long-game tutoring, he'd made me feel smart, special, sensational. And the kiss—sensual—

mouth on mouth—awakened parts of me that I had been trying to suppress. Good Christian girls didn't think about all the ways a person could indulge in matters of the flesh. At least, at the time I didn't think they should. This was a mistake, I was sure of it. But with boys my age, hadn't I let them touch me? Hadn't I experimented and wished for more, even as I'd shut down their advances when things got too close?

Yeah, but Jeff was married, and I was just a teenager with hormones igniting (that's why the illicit touching felt so good before it felt bad), and…

Here is the difficult part for me. This was not only about sex. Jeff was the first person (uh, *man*) who had ever made me feel like my thoughts, my ability to think and perceive, were interesting and worthy. We'd talk theology and faith and people stuff, and anything and everything that came to mind, and I had lots to say—and he listened. In the early going, that's what made me tolerate the first kiss and then want more. I'd come back, time and again, so that we could explore all the wonderful thoughts that were born of sinful sex.

"Tell me more," he'd say.

The encouragement became an aphrodisiac.

"I like what you say, Amy. I like being with you while your mind—my God, what a mind you have—runs free."

I was enthralled. He had found my weakness and was feeding me the very addictive drug of compliments.

In the beginning, we kissed on several occasions after spending time at the beach. He would brush his hand down my back or "accidently" graze my breasts after a hug that had lasted just a little too long, but the kind of hug I didn't want to end. I couldn't lose this support. It was essential to my being. I was afraid he would leave me if I didn't agree to some sort of intimacy. He was a vibrant, intelligent man who was married to a Christian woman who, so he claimed, denied him physical pleasure. Weren't married people supposed to have sex? If I denied his urges, he wouldn't want to spend time with me. Making love was not only the glue that kept us together, it was the will of God, or so Jeff said. He'd put it out there, and then I'd use it to justify my guilt.

"Amy, I know it sounds crazy, but I really feel like God has brought you into my life to give me comfort and love, so I can continue to tell other people about Jesus. You help restore me," he whispered.

Could that be true? The God I had been learning about wouldn't want that. Sure, maybe he had brought us together, but for an extramarital affair?

Punishment or protection?

This was wrong. But I wanted it so badly on so many levels. For starters, I just wanted to know what sex was all about. How did it feel? Where did it take you? Jeff loved and valued me. He wasn't like the boys I'd date, who might kiss and tell or brag in the locker room about feeling me up. No, Jeff couldn't tell anyone because he was a married Christian man, my Young Life leader, and was screwing a seventeen-year-old high school student.

So was my secret safe? Could I have as much sex as I wanted? Maybe no one would know, and then someday it would stop, and Jeff and I would go our separate ways. We'd go back to being a Young Life leader and his protégé. No harm done.

How naive! It had already had an impact on my life. I couldn't tell my girls on the swim team what was happening, and that may have affected the way I related. I couldn't tell my parents, nor would I ever tell the athletic director or my coach. What would they have thought? They wouldn't have understood. They would have wanted him arrested. Oh, to be able to go back and talk to myself and expose the truth around the story I had allowed myself to believe. That would come in time, just not then.

The touching eventually led to candle light and flower petals. After Jeff took my virginity, he cried, telling me how wrong our union was.

"Promise me, Amy, you'll never let me do this again."

Empowerment?

No. Manipulation.

Jeff made me feel like sex—to indulge or not to indulge—was my responsibility. And in a big way, it was. Just say no! I could allow it to happen or shut it down—a seventeen-year-old who had just been initiated into the pleasures of the flesh that went way beyond the physical glee she experienced as her long, beautiful body shot ahead of her competitors to win another race. Sex felt so much better than mere athleticism. Accomplishing goals in the pool was incredible; the freedom to express hidden desires was delectable.

So, after my virginity had been surrendered, what point was there in stopping? I was torn. Sex was like getting drunk without the hangover. It brought you closer to another person—not my girls on the relay team, but closer to Jeff, who said he adored me even while betraying a wife he described as simple and lacking my depth and complexity. She wasn't interested in pondering the depths of faith, he claimed. She was content with "Sunday school answers" to questions about God. She also didn't want to listen to him talk about his seminary classes, but I did.

This man also charmed me with love notes and songs he would write for me that he'd sing softly in his apartment, where we would meet. Our special world. I liked being with him so much I had to wonder if it really was so wrong. Maybe God had brought us together, even if theology and sexuality didn't mix so well.

Once after making love, lying together in the bed, limp, spent, fulfilled, Jeff whispered, "It never gets any better than this. You know that, right, Amy?"

All I knew was that it felt so good. I felt strong and sexy and beautiful, and wanton and wanted.

We continued through our very own summer of love, when I had lots of time on my hands because I was not working out in the pool. I was sexually satisfied, yet guilt wore on me as my encounters with Jeff became a regular part of my week. Eventually, I asked him about it.

"I think we should stop and get right with Jesus, don't you? This is hurting my relationship with God. I love being with you, but all the secrets and the lies hurt so bad."

Soon after, his lovemaking was not so gentle. One afternoon, after spending all day entwined in the sheets, he threw money on the bed and thanked me.

"It was a good time. Well worth the money."

Wait. What? We aren't making love anymore? We're just fucking? I thought I was special to you, but now you're telling me I'm your whore? You pay for the thrills?

I felt dirty and used. He said "role-playing" in bed was fun. But I didn't like the part I was expected to play. This didn't feel like love, and if it was kinky, it sure wasn't consensual. His lies—all the wooing and empty appreciation for my mind—had suddenly frayed. Yet he wouldn't let me leave him.

"Come on, Amy. I can't imagine living without you. I'll divorce my wife. I have to be with you."

"I don't believe you."

"You're precious to me. You're too important to—"

"No, Jeff. I should be with guys my own age. I should—"

"You know, if people find out, your family will hate you and you'll never be able to work for Young Life, right? You have to keep our secret. We would both be ruined for life—that is, if anyone believes you."

That scared me for real. In the beginning, after the first time, he had put me in control of our relationship.

Don't let me do it again. Now he was telling me that I couldn't say no.

That's when my personal integrity corralled me. Yeah, I'd felt the guilt and sometimes believed God would paint me with a scarlet letter for adultery and had feared I could be arrested for ruining a marriage. At seventeen I was "the other woman."

Now I was afraid my circle of peers, my family, my teachers would find out and hate me. I'd lose the respect of the people I loved. They thought I was innocent, and I knew I wasn't. This affair was every bit as much my secret to keep as it was Jeff's.

There was only one way out. College. My scholarship to swim at ISU, it would save me. It was my ticket out of this situation. I would have the protection of a tight meet schedule and wouldn't be able to come home. I would leave for school in late August and just not come back. I was desperate to be free of what had once liberated my body and soul. Now it felt like a vine that had entwined me, and the harder I struggled to free myself, the harder it choked me. It was easiest to simply stop struggling and await my escape to college.

## HOMEWARD BOUND

By evening, Ben had dropped me and our luggage at the Hartsfield-Jackson Atlanta International Airport and then sped away to return our rental car. I told myself I'd be fine, choosing to trust what my surgical team had told me: traveling home wouldn't be so bad.

Yet sitting caused so much pressure in my lower body that I felt like a water balloon ready to burst. So tight and full. I wanted to be drained of pain and discomfort.

The wheelchair Ben had arranged appeared, and I was rolled toward our gate. The overhead fluorescent lights were giving me a headache, and the hour's drive from the hotel had been long, so sitting in the wheelchair with my luggage clutched to my chest was nearly more than I could bear. I wanted to lay down. I needed to lay down. The taste of salt was in my mouth again; tears had escaped my eyes and spilled down my face. And this from a woman who had been pumped with narcotics.

I knew I had done everything possible to be as airport friendly as possible. I wore slip-on shoes; we had packed wisely. Now we took pains to explain to the female airport attendant who pushed my wheelchair that I had just had major surgery. Please be gentle. Please?

No way. She bolted down the hallways, hitting every bump along the way. When we finally arrived at the security checkpoint, I asked for my walker so I could walk through the metal detector. No go. I was told that the walker needed to be put through the X-ray machine—without me attached.

My blood began to warm in my veins. I was asked to stand up and walk through the checkpoint or sit in my wheelchair and surrender to a full-body pat down.

I gritted my teeth. "Pat me down, but I can't walk because I've just had surgery!"

Did anyone respond? Not that I recall. A tall thin woman with blue gloves came toward me and explained she was going to feel along my beltline and around my breasts and down my arms and legs.

"I've just had back surgery." I didn't bother trying to explain SI joint surgery. Who would get the significance of that?

The willowy woman wearing blue gloves nodded. I sensed some sympathy. Perhaps she was sorry, but she had a job to do, and she went about her business. I sat unblinking and rigid, pain and pressure bloating my lower half. Her hands explored my waistline and compressed my breasts. Why? It pissed me off. I was offended. My blood boiled. I wanted to scream, I am a human being!

Not that I felt like a person. I was the remains of a train wreck. A lump of worthless flesh. I turned my head to the side and waited for my pat down to be over. I reunited with Ben on the far side of security.

In the waiting area near our gate, I lay down on the floor to relieve the pressure and swallowed an anti-inflammatory muscle relaxant and two Percocet about thirty minutes prior to boarding. We also asked to be boarded last. The compassionate lady at the ticket desk moved a couple out of the spacious bulkhead seats so that we could sit there. I wished the TSA personnel had been as thoughtful.

When we landed in Normal, Illinois, I was quietly pleased that I had survived the flight. Only a ten-minute car ride and thirteen stairs were now between me and my bed.

At home I reunited with Connor and Erin amid squeals of joy and then looked up the stairway I had to climb.

"I'll carry you," Ben said.

"No."

"Amy…"

"Honey, thank you. But I didn't go under the knife so I could still be an invalid."

All eyes were on me as I ascended the stairs, my very own Mount Everest, holding tight to the banister. The twenty-minute climb drained me. Gingerly, I flopped into bed and slept soundly. I was home, but was I healed?

# Chapter 3

The college swim coaches were merciless during our workouts, which were long and arduous, beginning at 5:00 a.m. I'd never been so sore from physical exertion. While the schedule was not new, the training methods were. So much yardage.

The training structure was only part of the challenge.

Student-athletes attended athlete-approved classes, and every minute of our day felt like it was controlled and scheduled by the athletic department. I did not have a life in the normal sense of the word. Normal would have been strolling across campus with my book bag. The regimentation of the day made me feel like a military recruit, not a college student.

For example, athletes registered for classes before the general student body. And since some professors were not athlete friendly, there were teachers who were "approved" because they understood athletes must travel. I was frustrated when I couldn't enroll for a psychology class I wanted because it didn't fit the swim schedule. I didn't want "dumb" classes that were suggested for athletes so that they could easily keep their grades up. I was a student-athlete, not an athlete-student.

There were other advantages that seemed unfair. Food was more accessible in athletic dorms than regular dorms. We had special hours and less junk food. The university was catering to athletes, and the special treatment bugged me.

We also had to study and do homework in a monitored room just for athletes. This assured coaches that we were at least doing some homework. I had had more freedom as a senior in high school living with my parents than I did as a university athlete.

Then came some peer pressure from my teammates. The captains, seniors on the team, arrived at my dorm room encouraging me to gather with the girls at local bars, when all I wanted was to find time to attend a Bible study group. I needed to be around people who wanted to grow in their faith like I did. That would help me put the affair with Jeff behind me.

At one point, my coach said I was acting like I was better than everybody. The alienation was bad for team spirit. He encouraged me to hang out with the other girls. But I didn't want to go out drinking because I was only eighteen and we'd all signed contracts promising to conduct ourselves in a respectable manner.

This good-girl morality behavior had another down side. It seemed silly to resist alcohol after I had agreed to an affair with Jeff. There was no way I could explain to my teammates that I hoped the autumn semester would give me a fresh start away from my sinful relationship and selfish behaviors. Friendship would be an important part of my comeback, but not if it meant serious compromise. I craved emotional sustenance without the burden of a sexual relationship with a man who was older and supposedly wiser than me. Call me naive, but through prayer I was sure God could restore my relationship with Jeff to what it was supposed to be: mentor-protégé.

The strenuous August workouts prepared us for multiple tough weekend competitions that began in the fall. Between the swim meets, there was a lot of travel. Despite the challenges, I was thrilled to be a college-level swimmer, in part because my career had begun late in my youth when compared to other successful swimmers. Somehow I had made it to a Division I school and that made me proud, even though I was so tired my roommate Kelly would have to wake me up when I slept through the morning alarm clock.

In late October, I climbed onto the starting blocks for a relay race and thought, Wow, my back really doesn't feel right. I waited to see if it would go away. Later in the week, I told the coach, and he said not to worry about it, which didn't surprise me because by then I had come to the same conclusion as many scholarship athletes: you and your time are owned by the university.

"It doesn't sound like it's that bad, Amy. Just swim it off."

You have to trust your coach, right? He was far more experienced than I, and this was my first season swimming at a collegiate level. I ignored the inner voice telling me something wasn't right. When the starter beeped, I exploded off the blocks and completed my race.

At some point later—it could have been days or a couple weeks (our routines blurred the timelines)—I was in the pool working out, doing the yardage coach demanded of us. I was still stiff and sore but not complaining. As I approached the end of the pool, I performed the same flip turn all swimmers know well. But this one was different. I don't think anyone in or around the pool heard it because it was internal. The loud snap of a rubber band followed by white-hot pain in the right side of my pelvis. To this day, I remember it like the graphics displayed on television screens during Batman fight scenes: Zap! Ka-pow! Bam!

My body was unceremoniously yanked from the pool; by whom I don't remember. I suppose he thought I needed saving, and I suppose he was right. My athletic body no longer functioned. Had I been alone, I doubt I could have pulled myself from the water.

A trainer began stretching my legs, which caused excruciating pain. I shouted, "Oh my God, stop! Don't touch me!"

After that I don't have clear memories. Not because I blacked out. I'd been arrested by disorienting and searing pain, and I was overcome by a layer of panic. What happens now?

It would be six months of scary, lonely appointments with doctors, therapists, and trainers before I knew that I would never again swim in an NCAA competition.

## ONE WEEK AFTER SURGERY

I woke up to the smell of coffee, and that was nice, but I needed more medication. My sense was that things were improving and all would be right soon, but only if I had drugs in me. Meds were a must because the minute their magic wore off, I would plunge into the depths of despair. The pain was strong, and it felt like my entire body was congested and as heavy as concrete. In those moments, it would take every ounce of energy not to freak out and panic. Had I done something stupid, dear Lord? The worry itself was draining. Increased pain had always represented increased damage or injury to me. The fear of screwing up the surgery was overwhelming.

Linda, my mother-in-law from Florida, was another form of salvation. She gladly loved the kids and ran the household while Ben and I were out of state for the medical procedure. Then she stayed on until my own parents could arrive and relieve her of her duties, such as making a great cup of morning joe and delivering all my home-cooked meals. I was still not able to care for myself and had no interest in the ritual of getting dressed each day. Sleeping, drinking water, and breathing were all I could manage.

Linda also protected me from the never-ending needs of my kids. I missed my kiddos, but I couldn't even fake a caring, protective attitude. Even listening to their mile-a-minute stories with a smile sucked the wind from my sails. I didn't have any reserves; I had nothing to give but dearly wanted to. After spending time with them, I'd feel exhausted, even though they were just excited to see me. That killed me. I felt twisted. I needed protection from my own kids?

But even a short trip to the bathroom was the equivalent of a decathlon: my pulse raced, I gulped for air, and my body collapsed across the finish line—my bed.

It made me mad. Why was it so freaking hard? Linda understood. Her wise counsel helped me accept my fate as a helpless, bedridden mother.

"You need food and sleep; the rest will come eventually," she said whenever I voiced my frustration. "You need to give yourself this time. You need to not worry about everybody else. OK?"

Fully knowing I'd be spending a lot of time in our bedroom, Ben had set it for long-haul convalescence. He used equipment my parents had loaned us: a walker; a handheld shower nozzle in the shower; a shower chair; and, my favorite, a raised toilet seat. They'd also sent us a foam triangle bolster to lift my knees and flatten my lower back and a laptop PC table for me to use in bed. The additions had a definite nursing home vibe, but who could complain? My friends had helped dull the institutional look by painting the walls a honeydew hue that surrounded me with hopes of a spring awakening. The color would see me through my winter of discontent, both seasonal and figurative.

And let's not forget the six-month subscription to Netflix provided by my brother-in-law. I was surrounded by good intentions. Now if only my body would respond and cooperate.

Meaningful victories soon arrived.

The first time I could walk from bed to bathroom without my walker—one step for womankind!—was a good omen. Standing unassisted long enough to wash my face and brush my teeth was gratifying. And finally, after a long sleep, I awoke, and the pain wasn't quite as unbearable as it had once been. Not that my body had yet forgiven the doctor who had recently cut into my rear end and tightened five screws. But after the lower back pain I'd experienced for eighteen years, I felt like a rose about to bloom.

On the other hand, maybe my post-op painkillers really were effective. I'd taken my medicine as prescribed, on and off, for years with very little relief. It had been frustrating, and the cost of prescription and over-the-counter medications had added up. I couldn't understand why anyone would bother using the usual suspects, name brands that were no more helpful than gulping aspirin, to fight cancer. The fact that my prescription meds were doing the job should have been a clue to me as to how much pain I had been in through the years. Mental note, Amy: morphine—"the most important narcotic and addictive principle of opium," according to Dictionary.com—was just about the only substance that managed your agony when administered in the hospital.

I was beginning to put some things in perspective. The epic power of denial and the role of the human mind had played large roles in my travail. Just how persuasive and intricate they had been would not be clear to me for another year or more. But even a week after surgery, I could not help but recall the many doctors who had told me the MRIs and other tests had revealed no problem with my hips, lower back, or pelvis. The pain is all in your head. Some alternative medical professionals might agree. There is no such thing as pain. It's all mental. Yet for nearly two decades, I had been trapped between crippling back and butt pain and the confusing idea that I was inventing and exaggerating the impact of an injury.

Had I been mad? Just another "hysterical" female who could not cope with life?

Apparently not. The Facebook support group I had joined before surgery had opened my eyes. That's when I had learned that I was not alone. I had engaged with other women and men who had also been suffering from chronic pain and who had been very supportive of me. Proof that I had not been the only one on the medical merry-go-round of questionable consultations, unclear treatment paths, and obsolete medical guidelines.

While in Georgia meeting with the physician, and later when I had entered the hospital for the surgery, I had avidly updated the Facebook group because I had promised to document every step of the process.

## WHAT IS THIS?

After my injury in the pool, movement was difficult. I couldn't drive, and walking was terribly painful. I also could not sit at a classroom desk. As a result, I was forced to lie on my back on the floor with my legs propped up on the seat of a chair. All notes were taken in pencil because my position confounded the flow of ink. I should have contacted NASA and asked to borrow a space pen. In fact, floating in outer space sounded good.

My initial doctor was condescending, the first in a long line of medical professionals who would not take my pain seriously. "We couldn't find anything. It must be in your head."

This medical opinion gave birth to a demeaning, destructive narrative: She didn't want to swim. Faking an injury was her way out. My pain wasn't real because no one could find it in an image.

Stopping my classroom studies was not an option. My goal was to become a teacher, and I would not be derailed from that achievement. At the very least, I had to find a way to get through the school year.

I saw the athletic trainer, John Munn, a couple of times a week just to get the pain under control. John believed me. He had compassion for the magnitude of the injury and the stakes for me. His genuine empathy convinced me he wanted to heal my young, wrecked body. Over eighteen years, he would be one of only three professional men who would validate me and do everything in their power to restore me.

Lack of guidance was another part of my downfall. My parents did not recognize the seriousness of the injury and so assumed I could handle recovery on my own. Also, the university was of no help, other than allowing me to work with John for a few months. This was the first time I had ever tried to navigate a serious health challenge, and my naivete was boundless. When I was being prepared for a CT bone scan, an IV needle was inserted into my arm so that radioactive isotopes could swim in my body and reveal fractures. The technician wore a protective lead vest, but I did not. But the package was marked with a green skull and crossbones that indicated the fluid was poisonous. How could this be healthy? Why didn't they explain it to me? Informed consent. No—uninformed consent.

Through it all, I was accompanied by Kelly, the junior high school friend who had become my college roommate. Her kindness went beyond the call of duty and included driving me north to Chicago—a five-hour round trip—on weekends. My high school athletic director had referred me to a physical therapist, Anne, who helped athletes. This was late December 1992. My visits continued into the following year.

Anne was the first health professional to diagnose the cause of my pain. "Amy, your sacroiliac is out of place because you've torn your ligaments. That was probably the pop you heard in the pool. That made your pelvis unstable."

Sacroiliac joint dysfunction (SIJD). It would not be the last time I would hear this name. Anne explained how the sacroiliac joint connects the sacrum and the two ilia (our pelvic bones), which link the pelvis to the lower spine. It did not surprise me that the SI joint, at both sides of the pelvis, was essential for transferring forces though the upper and lower body.

Just identifying the issue felt like progress. For the first time, I had hope. The PT didn't think I was crazy. It was extremely uplifting validation that all this was not merely in my head. My lower back pain was similar to what she'd seen in other women. I was ecstatic.

"But will I get better? Can you fix me?" I was afraid of the answer.

"Let's get started. There is room for improvement; I believe we can make progress. We'll make the best attempt. I've seen this in others, and they got better. I believe we can make this better, but it will always be a bit of a problem for you," she said.

On the drive home, Kelly could tell I was in a funk, even after hearing supposedly encouraging news. "What's wrong?"

My answer was bitter. "Men."

"Yeah?"

"They kind of suck, don't they?"

She turned up the Allman Brothers on the radio, and we sped south. Her silence allowed me to stew. I knew that I didn't want to become "that woman," the resentful ball-busting female figure who blamed everything gone wrong on the other gender. I struggled to even my keel so that I could sail into friendlier streams of thought.

John, the trainer, collaborated with my physical therapist to develop a plan that would help control my pain and get me on my feet. He was a good man. By late winter, I could sit up in class for short periods and tolerate short walks across campus. I was healing and beginning to believe I might be able to live a normal-ish life, though it probably wouldn't include a lot of high adventure. Anne reminded me of my alignment and instability issues during each of her sessions; I was waiting to be strong enough to hold my pelvis in place on its own. The pain was improving, but I was still presenting with rotations. I was still icing a lot and taking meds to manage the pain.

# Chapter 9

Mealtimes were hard for me. I'd hear my family gathered around the dinner table while I was marooned in my bed. Sometimes it was too much, like my heart might burst. I was all too aware that I was missing out on the lives of people I dearly loved because it hurt so much to walk the stairs and sit at the table to eat.

I struggled to remind myself what I had been told: When it hurt more, rest. Don't do the things that hurt; limit your activities. I had obeyed that so often I wasn't sure what remained that I could do, and the isolation of being in my bedroom prison tower while my family lived around me was torture.

After shaking away the mental anguish, I often reminded myself that the doctors knew best. Yet as soon as I said this to myself, I would hear another voice whisper, *But do they?*

The doubt trailed me like a shadow. Was lying still and not moving really helping me? If so, why was it taking so long to improve? Was I really so fragile?

I couldn't help but consider these questions because it hurt almost as much while I was lying in bed as it did while I sat at the kitchen table. What was the best thing?

Did the doctors and therapists mean to reduce my life to such a limited existence in this one room? Were they secretly saying I would never be capable of living a larger, more active life?

After my surgery, I decided getting well meant that I had to listen to my body and try to partner with it. Maybe I should be a little kinder to it rather than ignore its every complaint and just order it around like an indentured servant—do this, do that—without regard for the warnings or information my body was trying to give me. Making the change was not easy because the slogans that had covered my swim T-shirts, locker rooms, and bedroom while growing up were an integral part of the way I understood pain. They had been the foundation of my simple adolescent philosophy of life:

"No pain, no gain."

"The pain you feel today is the strength you feel tomorrow."

"If you're going through hell, keep going."

And my favorite, "Pain is temporary, *pride* is forever."

The idea that I should never quit, never give up, and never give in to defeat meant that there was always more that I could and should do to succeed. Do it faster; do it harder; do it more and more. Those thoughts were so ingrained that as an adult recovering from surgery, I realized I didn't know how to listen to my body. I hadn't even known that I needed to. As an athlete, I had learned to push my body to extremes, to the point of exhaustion, and then do it all over again the next day in the pool. It had never occurred to me that I might need to find a different mental attitude if I was going to make progress in reducing my pain and ever be able to return to the things I missed so much.

To some degree, the demands I put on myself sprung from my fear that I might lose even more of the things that made me *me*. Slowly, I began to realize that it was not only my body that needed to heal. I had to slow down long enough to examine my guiding thoughts and beliefs.

*Why must everything be so hard, Venus?*

It has been said that the secret of change is to focus all your energy not on fighting the old but on building the new. Socrates. I knew that was right, but the practicality of it would take a long time to implement. After you've done a thing the same way for two years, look it over carefully. After five years, look at it with suspicion. And after ten years, throw it away and start all over. Alfred Edward Perlman. So I told myself I had to stop focusing on all the things that frightened and freaked me out.

*Yeah, yeah, I know; everything aches, Amy, even when you're just lying in bed and both legs twitch and spasm for reasons you can't understand. You feel weak beyond words even when trying to walk to the bathroom. Yeah, I know, Amy. And your hyper focus on the sensations (so that you can tell the doctors what's going on) when you feel weakness in your backside, hips, and hamstrings is commendable, but…it also means you begin to experience that heavy feeling, like something dark is sitting on your chest. It makes it hard to breath. And you hate that feeling more than just about anything, right? So put your focus on something positive.*

Good advice, because I always felt better when I discovered small wins. For example, when I realized I could sit upright in a chair for fifteen to thirty minutes a few times a day without wanting to amputate my right side from the butt to my knee! Also, as much as I had appreciated and needed the medications, when I cut back on the pain meds without any increase in my discomfort, I nodded to myself and said, "Cool."

Regardless of my attempts at being positive, I still experienced anxiety. *Please let this surgery be the thing that finally works to end my pain*, I would pray.

Maybe my worries were just ingrained habits. If I thought more positively, could I think away this pain? That idea seemed insulting and impossible. I wouldn't have pain if I could think my way out of it. So I jammed that thought in the trash bin. It sounded too much like those medical professionals who believed I had made up my pain. Why in the world would I make up pain?

After years of managing the relentless pain, it was difficult to steer my focus away from every little twitch and sensation. I began to see it would take a long time before my mind and body could accept that things could be different now. One moment my mind would be full of hopeful thoughts. Then suddenly it would attack, and I'd be back in the headspace that had defined my days before the surgery, crazy with stress, fear of losing my family life, and the terrible sense that my decision to undergo the procedure was a mistake. The despair had been overwhelming. I'd burst into tears. I couldn't revisit those suicidal days and longer nights. Hopelessness brings one to dark corners. I just couldn't go back. Sobbing, I'd say, "This has to work!"

Near the end of my first week at home, I was entertaining the idea of resuming physical therapy. Part of me was going stir-crazy. An extravert in the role of a shut-in was fraying my nerves. Social media like Facebook was a godsend, but I wanted to *live* in my world again, be normal, and spend time with people face-to-face. To make that change, I needed the kind of reassurance that Tim, my physical therapist, had always provided me. When I felt emotionally weak all alone in my bedroom, in my mind I would replay what he had said before my trip to Georgia for the surgery.

"Aim, it took eighteen years to get here. When you get back from surgery, how about you give me a month for every year before we get worried? Or at least give me a full year. Can you do that for me? You and me with a plan; we got this. It's gonna be good, I know it."

I'd been referred to Tim more than two years before my surgery and after more than a decade and a half of riding the medical merry-go-round of vague diagnoses and even more vague treatment plans. But after we'd worked together for about nine months, Tim had sat me down and had a come-to-Jesus talk with me: he would have to discharge me from physical therapy for "failure to progress."

"I know you're doing everything I ask of you, but the pain isn't changing, Aim. We have to be objective. When your menstrual cycle comes, I feel like we are back at square one, and you're strong—crazy strong…" His voice trailed off. "But there's nothing more I can do for you."

He had looked down at the table, defeated. Something in my mind had exploded—I had been back in the dingy swim office. I had felt like I was being left alone again. I had lost the ground I had gained. I would be losing my ally. He had touched my arm to refocus me; it had worked. I had snapped back to the conversation at hand. He had said I needed to consider other options.

"What other options?"

"Well, you could look into prolotherapy, or consult with a surgeon. Aim, I can't tell you what to do. That's not for me to decide; all I can tell you is that I can't fix you."

He had been heartbroken. After all, we had both remembered the enthusiasm he had brought to the process and the humbling words he had uttered at the start: "You're going to be my Venus de Milo. You know who she is?"

"The statue of the chick with no arms?"

He had laughed, then said, "This will be my best work. You'll be my masterpiece!"

It had not been Tim's fault that he had had to discharge me like so many others. I had known therapy hadn't been making me better, but it *had* been keeping me from getting worse. The manipulations, stretching, strengthening and massage he had done were not things I could have done on my own, even though he had taught me many ways to care for myself and had even given Ben a few pointers. Admitting defeat had been hard for both of us.

"I'm sorry, Amy."

Although Tim had felt like a failure, that had not been how I had seen it. He had accurately identified the pain in my SI joint. He had also helped me understand and accept that it had been time for a new approach. By that point I had trusted him implicitly; he had been my medical voice of reason, and his insights had been accurate. He had also known me as well as any health practitioner could have. Through asking perceptive questions, he had understood my deepest fears and emotional tipping points.

"I know these next steps are scary, but I've tried everything; you've tried everything. Surgery is just the next logical step to look into," he had finally said.

But had it been?

Tim had never explained *why* PT hadn't been enough, so I could only assume my pelvis had been too damaged and unstable to fix conservatively. Then I had had to figure out what surgeon to trust and decide what procedure would be best for me. I had felt alone again; I had fought back tears.

Tim broke the silence. "You know you can always email or call me and bounce ideas off me, right? I'm still going to be here."

Something in his tone had let me know he had *really* meant it.

After that conversation, it had taken ten months to do my research and choose among the available options and decide what made the most sense at that time. I'd enlisted good people who would act as my postoperative recovery team. They had included a pain management physician and my primary care doctor, who would oversee any labs and imaging that were needed. He would also prescribe my physical therapy so that I could keep working with Tim. After all, Tim had promised to restore me. He had deserved a second chance. And so had I.

## THE ITCH

When I had had chicken pox as a ten-year-old kid, I had had sores all over my body, down my throat, and I recall I had even had them on the backs of my eyelids. I'd sit in a bathtub full of pink, chalky calamine lotion trying not to scratch every itchy inch of my body. It had been the most irksome experience I had ever had.

Until my surgery.

I had four single stitches on my backside that were narrower than my pinky fingernail—and they itched worse than a body full of chicken pox. I was told that was a good sign. It meant the skin was healing. But how long was it gonna take?

And then there was the iodine that still streaked my butt and lower back. The sponge baths I had had during my hospital stay were just not helping me feel civilized. Now that I had been home a few days, I realized I was afraid of the wet, slippery shower. My fear was that I would slip and fall on my Bambi legs or the wet floor and mess up the screws that rested deep in my bones and held my SI joint together. This thought made me seriously risk averse, even while under the influence of narcotics.

I was feeling optimistic when Ben walked into our bedroom, and I said, "I think I'd like to take a shower; can you help me do that?"

"Of course I can." He disappeared around the corner, and I heard clatter and then the spray of water hitting the shower seat.

It took enormous effort to roll over, get out of bed, walk to the bathroom—which was less than twenty steps away—and get undressed. He helped steady me as I stepped over the four-inch lip into the shower, where I carefully lowered my body onto the chair my mom had loaned us. My emotional stability plummeted.

Mere moments ago, I had been so excited about taking a shower. I had even thought I might be able to manage the task alone. Within three minutes, that hope had been dashed. Independent self-care, I realized, was impossible. My mind raced. *Why can't I do this?* My surgeon had said most people who have the surgery return to physical therapy about three weeks after the procedure and go back to work between three and eight weeks. How in the world? No way. The pain was still so intense, and it all felt so hard. I dropped my eyes and could not meet Ben's gaze.

Few words were spoken as my husband gently washed away the grime and antiseptic stains. Then he knelt and tenderly, humbly began to shave my legs. Was this how the leper had felt when Jesus had touched him?

Overwhelmed by the respect the Son of God had shown him?

I felt unworthy of the loving gesture. I couldn't cook or clean; I couldn't pick up the kids after their activities. The truth was I hadn't been able to do any of those things for far longer than I cared to admit. Years. Long, painful years of dependence. What if that never changed?

Ben reached forward, and I extended my hand, expecting him to steady me as I stood. Instead, he dropped a dollop of shampoo into my palm.

"Why don't you wash your hair, and I'll get you a clean change of clothes?"

A meek smile spread across my face. "OK."

He left me under the shower spray for a few minutes. As I was rinsing my hair, he returned. "You want me to take your stitches out now?"

"Yes!"

My head was such a crazy mess. Terror and depression in one moment and elation the next. The emotional swings were almost as exhausting as the physical labor of showering.

## UNFORGIVEN

After my college swimming accident and before meeting for the first time with my physical therapist in Chicago, I had gone home to see my parents during winter break. This had been the first time they'd seen me since hearing about my injury. They had had no idea that I was moving like a crooked and crippled ninety-year-old woman. Shocked, Dad had suggested I visit our family doctor. That had turned out to be another medical fiasco involving an injection that had proven useless at anything other than increasing my pain.

But by the early spring of 1993, after about four months with Anne, her guidance had me walking more like myself, although less confident and more self-conscious of my posture. She'd given me an SI belt, which she had explained would brace and stabilize the SI joint, which would help the ligaments to heal. The belt certainly provided a sense of security while I went about my day and performed the exercises I'd been taught to activate and strengthen muscles in my core. She kept telling me the glute muscles were being lazy.

I admit there were times I simply didn't know how to internalize this information. I was the strongest I had ever been at the time of my injury. I was dropping time and lifting more in the weight room than I ever had, so how could I be so weak? I could squat 1.5 times my body weight; I could bench my body weight; I had abs of steel; you could bounce quarters off them and my rear end! How was I not strong enough after all those achievements?

I just didn't get it, so mentally I shrugged those thoughts away because at the end of the day, I felt better when Anne worked her magic with her hands. She had also given me ways to manage my pain between sessions. When she would discharged me, I would be free of pain most of the time, with the exception of my menstrual cycle.

She was the professional; she was getting results no one else had. She had given me a reason for my pain. She had listened to my story and my fears. She had calmed me and therefore my nervous system and given me confidence. I'll always be grateful for the help, even if at times her explanations of my condition were confusing and some well-meaning suggestions would lead to unintended consequences.

For example, after my injury, my menstrual cycle had arrived with insane pain that had lasted for a few days and then faded. Anne had recommended that I take birth control pills to stop my cycle until my lower back could heal. This had sent me to student health services on campus. I had been so naive I hadn't realized what personal information they would need.

"Are you sexually active?" a nurse had asked.

I had blushed and stuttered. This had been the first time I had ever admitted to anyone that I was not a virgin. Visions of Jeff and I in bed had passed through my mind. I had admonished myself: *Don't think about that. You are friends now, not lovers.* That *part of the relationship is over.*

"Uh, yes. Sort of. I mean I *was*, but…"

"OK. In that case we'll need to screen you for STDs."

Sexually transmitted diseases? It had never dawned on me that Jeff might have shared more than pleasure with me. We had never used protection. He had said he didn't like the way it felt…*Oh, Amy, you idiot!* Of course my mind had run rampant with all the possibilities. *I might have HIV!* But in the deep, dark recesses of my mind, I had wondered if my former lover had been having sex with other girls. For the first time, it had dawned on me that I might not have been the only one. I might not have been as special as he had said I was. What if he had been lying to me? What if…? The thought had been so horrible I had pushed it away. No, this hadn't been abuse; it had been an affair. It had been consensual. It had been wrong, but I had said yes, hadn't I?

Waiting for the test results had been agonizing and stressful. Thank God, he had not "gifted" me anything.

By the end of my freshman year I'd improved to the point where Anne could discharge me. But at the end of our work, some of her advice bothered me. First, I was told that it was time to hang up my goggles and swim cap; I should not swim competitively again. To be fair, this conclusion had been echoed by several medical professionals, and I had mostly accepted it, even though I had never understood it.

Next, I was told I would likely need surgery someday, so keep that idea on my radar. Anne explained there was a surgery available that would fuse my joints together, but she hoped in time there would be a way to instead repair the injured ligaments surgically. But unfortunately the surgical interventions just weren't there yet.

"Remember, Amy: it's not the joint; it's your damaged ligaments."

Sadly, I would never forget this explanation given for my pain.

Finally, what hurt most was hearing that I probably should not have children. "Be careful about pregnancy. Your body may not be able to handle the burden."

I rejected the idea immediately. *No. I'm going to be a mom. You can't take that future from me too!* At the time, my stubborn conviction about having children was mostly wishful thinking and to some degree a reaction to another painful loss I had endured in that same month.

Illinois State University had revoked my swimming scholarship.

When I had learned about the decision, my frustrations and fears for the future had been replaced with a mixture of depression and rage. And it had all been directed at my coach. He hadn't given a damn about me. I had been of no value to him if I couldn't swim.

Despite the teachings of my Christian faith, I had loathed him and could not find one forgiving impulse in me. He had never shown that he had cared about my injury or my person. He hadn't given a hoot that my career had been ruined, although he'd given me all kinds of attention during the recruiting process. *You'll be a great addition to the team. We've got to have you.* I had been disgusted with the whole thing. They win you over, then essentially enslave you. I had felt no more human than a circus animal who was no longer able to perform in the big show and was discarded and sent to pasture.

For months after the "snap" that had ended my swimming career, I'd labored to bring myself to a place of balance and good health. I'd made good on my vow to distance myself from Jeff and had prayed to God to make everything right within me. Yet it would take years to process my final encounters with my coach after the university's ruling. Sitting at a desk in a dank, dingy athletic office, my coach had shoved the papers for ending my athletic relationship with ISU toward me and said, "If you don't want to swim, just sign."

If I'd had a knife, I had known exactly where I would have plunged it. His heart would have been in the palm of my hand moments later. I'd have gutted him just so he could know how empty, helpless, and forsaken he had made me, a scholarship athlete, feel when he had callously uttered, *If you don't want to swim…*

But I hadn't had the strength to defend myself or lash out. I had felt like I was the one who had been stabbed. My body had shaken like a runaway train, cascading downhill and heading for a turn that would force it off the tracks. Sobs had echoed in the squalid office, which had stunk of pool chemicals and pity. Tears had stained the document. With pen in hand, I had signed away my dreams.

Years later, when I was researching the surgery Tim had advised me to consider, I reached out to my former coach with the hope that the university had new resources he could share concerning back pain. Perhaps another swimmer had experienced something similar to my pain, and new solutions and doctors had been discovered.

I popped into the pool facility one day and approached him in his on-deck office. We were face-to-face for the first time in a long time. He looked at me and said, "You're still dealing with that problem?"

"Yes."

"Huh," he muttered. "No. No new ideas." His face was blank and devoid of empathy or concern.

And then he turned and walked away. *Men.* At least his inability to sympathize or ask questions or show some compassion reinforced that the sense of loss I had experienced in the spring of 1993 had not been self-pity or immaturity. I recalled that day so long ago. I had been lost and low, despite attempts by new college friends and roommate Kelly to console me. I had wanted comfort. I had wanted not to feel alone. I had desperately wanted to be listened to, understood, and supported.

Throughout my freshman year, Jeff and I had stayed in contact. He had called regularly to talk with me; written loving, supportive letters; and anonymously sent flowers to my dorm room. Throughout my time in pain, he had courted me, though he had never pressured me for sex. I had been relieved by his restraint, until my loneliness had made me pick up the phone and dial. He had answered quickly, as if he had known it was me.

"Jeff?"

"Hey, I'm glad you called. I've missed you!"

"I really need to see you…"

"I've been waiting to hear you say that," he had said.

# Chapter 5

I needed pain medications to survive the surgery. No one in his or her right mind would doubt that. Yet as I lay on my bed healing, I pondered the many doctors throughout my eighteen-year ordeal who had all but accused me of being a junkie. To them I had been a paragon of health and had not needed pain medications. They had concluded, after one more MRI or scan or X-ray, that I had made the appointment only because I had been addicted to pills and hoped I could get another prescription.

Yet they all had said I was fine and nothing was wrong.

I had fought it at first.

"You are fine."

I would start sweetly and kindly. "No, please listen."

"Amy, there is nothing on your X-ray to indicate—"

My jaw would tighten. "Doctor, I have low back pain due to a sacroiliac joint problem."

"Oh?"

"Yes. I injured it when I was a competitive swimmer, and it gets so bad I can't manage it on my own. I need…"

When their eyes would cloud over, my voice would trail off. I'd be told how young and vibrant and healthy I looked.

"You're such a pretty girl, such a smart girl. Your spine looked fantastic."

My anger would occasionally burst as I would labor to explain that my spine was not in question.

"Just look at my pelvis, the SI joint. *Please.*"

The response would be the same. I'd be told that it would take massive forces to disrupt those ligaments. "They're strong enough to hold a car, you know."

Yes, I knew. Except my PT had explained they were injured and torn and wouldn't heal, so mine were different, you see. The doctors would shake their heads in disbelief. I would wonder how they could not know these things; they were MDs with fancy credentials. Surely, they should know more than a PT. Years later I would finally understand why this had been such a common response. The PTs knew more than I had ever given them credit for. It's too bad this information had been communicated by a variety of health professionals in such a demeaning and unsupportive manner.

I'd had many negative encounters with doctors disbelieving my pain. They had thought I wanted opioids, when I all had been asking for were muscle relaxants. I had been so weary of being seen as a pill popper. I had learned to arrive at the health offices unkempt. I'd use makeup foundation a shade lighter than my natural skin color, or I'd use powder to make my complexion less rosy.

One medical professional had advised me to add a darker hue under my eyes to make me look haggard. The idea had been to avoid looking too healthy because apparently women who occasionally smile or laugh cannot possibly have a serious problem with pain.

The whole charade had been demeaning, infuriating, and ultimately heartbreaking. I would discover that the only way to get what I needed at the time—just muscle relaxants!—was to follow these rules:

1. Always wait six months or longer between visits.

2. Skip the ER and go to prompt care clinics instead.

3. It's OK to ask for muscle relaxants, but don't ask for opioids.

4. Never rate your pain as a ten out of ten or higher. Choose seven or eight on a scale of ten, and people will pay attention and believe you.

5. Only use these meds sparingly, when the pain is unbearable. Then guard the rest with your life.

This method had allowed me to make those precious meds last. I had had to have ammunition in the event of a horrible day. I had prayed that if I knocked myself out with a cocktail and my muscle relaxants that I'd be able to recover and go back to my regular life after a day or two.

Sadly, even with my rules of desperation in place, I had suffered often and rarely found anyone who would hear me out and help me. So much for the oath to "do no harm."

Then one day I had decided to speak to my kids' general practitioner.

Dr. James Hancock had been one of a few helpful and caring medical professionals I had met during my long journey. He had been easy to talk to, encouraged questions, and explained things in a way that was refreshing.

Also, he had never talked down to me as a parent, and he had been truthful when unsure of next steps. When Erin had been five, she had been in pain, and it had turned out to be her appendix. Dr. Hancock had assessed her and known she was not presenting as "normal." He had assured us our instincts had correct, but he had not felt comfortable making a definitive decision, so he had set up an appointment with a surgeon. Erin had had her appendix removed that night. Ever since, I had trusted him.

Two years before my surgery, I had told him my whole story, starting all the way back with my swimming injury in 1992. I had come armed with medical articles to back up what I was saying, and he had listened and listened, and when I had finished, he had stated simply and clearly, "I know what is going on with your health. I know what you need and how I can help."

Relief? An understatement. A doctor who had not only listened but wanted me to partner with him in finding solutions. Priceless!

We had agreed he would manage and prescribe my pain medications. And he had assured me that all I would need to do when in pain was to call and come in to see him, and he would help. My trust in him had been well placed, and all had gone very well—until the day he had been out of town and I had needed immediate attention.

On that visit, I had met with another doctor. I had walked in hopeful and left demoralized and barely able to walk—not that I had been walking all that well when I had arrived. I had hobbled into the office and obediently gotten onto the treatment table.

The questions he had asked had been easy to answer. Where had the pain been? When had it been worse? Typical stuff that I'd responded to hundreds of times.

"This is a chronic problem," I had said. "I'm looking into surgical options, but I need time to do the research. Dr. Hancock agreed to manage my case and medications."

As soon as he had turned stern with me and mentioned the need to do some testing, I had known I was in trouble.

"I'm not just handing out narcotics," he had snarled.

Ah, great. The junkie insinuation. He had recommended "great" anti-inflammatory patches and creams and said I would be welcome to samples. I had not been enthused. In the previous two freakin' decades, I'd tried every cream, pill, patch, and wonder treatment available. I had wanted to say, "Yeah, sure, Doc. Bring it on. Let's try some creams—or no, wait, why don't you just give me a Band-Aid and kiss it to make it all better?"

I had been pissed off and having trouble hiding it.

"OK, let's do those tests," he had said.

Tears had begun to gather.

"What are you going to do?" I had already known the results from the standard tests I had endured. I had also known that if I could keep him from doing the provocation testing to prove my pain I might avoid further injury and be able to drive home. Otherwise I would most likely have to call someone to come get me.

I had run through the test names and the results he would get from them in hopes of convincing him I had known what I had been talking about. I had begged him to call Tim, my physical therapist, for confirmation so the tests wouldn't be needed. I had been desperate—desperate for him *not* to bother.

"You seem to know all the 'right' answers," he had said.

So I would be punished for being informed? I had just not been able to win. Fury had heated up in me. My pain levels had been about to be escalated—again—by yet another arrogant physician.

He had begun the tests that required manipulating the position of my legs, but he hadn't been as gentle as Tim. I had cried out in pain, and the tears had begun to flow.

By then I had been a category-four hurricane ready to pound him. He had gotten the message, and his face had softened. Had he looked apologetic? Yes. He had cast his eyes downward.

"Let me get you a prescription for pain meds, Valium to help you sleep, and a muscle relaxant. I'll give you a bunch of the cream samples too, in case it helps." He had walked out of the room.

Had he learned anything? If another woman had arrived the next week with the same complaints, would he have been any more cautious or humane? He had been a licensed, experienced doctor who had had no idea what he had just provoked in my body, except that it had not been what he had expected.

He had returned, handed me the scripts and samples, and told me I was free to go. *Well, thank you. What are you, the prison warden? Free to go. Yeah, sure.*

"That's not going to be so easy," I had said through gritted teeth and spittle from suppressed rage. I had barely been able to get off the treatment table before I had begun my hobble out of the office—a lot worse than the hobble that had brought me in.

As he had watched me drag my right leg behind me, I had heard an astonished, "Did I do that?"

Steely and unforgiving, I had barely looked at him. "Yes. I really wish you had believed me, *Doctor*."

In my car I had sat and cried for thirty minutes before I could attempt to drive. I had been on my own. The entire trip home I had prayed that I would not need to slam on the brakes or swerve to avoid another vehicle. For days after that appointment, I had been useless.

## COLD TURKEY

Two weeks after surgery, I stopped taking my pain medications. I had no idea if going cold turkey was a good idea, but I needed to assess where I was in my recuperation. I'd noticed in the previous few days that I had been using the meds not so much to relieve pain as to increase my mobility and get more done during the day. Also, I was tired of feeling disconnected from my emotions and thoughts. I was grateful for the sophisticated medications that kept my pain under control, but I was ready to rejoin reality and stop living under their influence like a brainless zombie.

I had done nothing those last fourteen days but lie in bed, staring at the television or computer or sleeping. Life was passing me by, and I was eager to get out of my bedroom. With that in mind, I kept going over what the surgical team had told me: many people can go back to work three to six weeks after the operation. If I was going to get there, I would have to start pushing myself to get better, not just lie around worrying that I might reinjure myself. The three-week mark was only seven days away.

What was wrong with me? It was a question I could not help but ask. I was still in bed most of the day. Was I a slacker? It was getting scary to think too long about my situation. Didn't I have to start reclaiming my life?

Physical therapy was scheduled to resume the following week, and my seventy-six-year-old dad reminded me of his hip replacement surgery and his fast post-op recovery. "Heck, by this point I was going up and down stairs with alternating feet, Amy," he said all too often for my liking.

His comments made their mark and sometimes got me thinking that maybe I was worse off than before the surgery. Too often I felt hopelessly broken. Maybe all the king's men really couldn't put Humpty-Dumpty back together again.

That was insane, of course. The truth was my pre-op life had been largely faked. I had pretended that I could get through daily activities. To the casual onlooker, or others I would interact with for short periods outside my home, I might have appeared to be a normal mom and wife. Nonsense. If you'd spent long periods of time with me, you would have eventually witnessed my dysfunction.

Honestly, looking back I couldn't remember many of the special moments in my children's lives. Oh, I had sat through many scouting events, school sings, swim meets, and so forth, but I had been hopped up on meds just so I could technically be present and my children would have memories of my presence.

Heart-wrenching.

The reality was that it had been hard to be anywhere when I had had to constantly plan one step ahead. How many steps would it take to get from point A to point B? How many stairs would I have to climb, and were handrails on those staircases? Would I have places to lean or sit for a rest?

The other challenges had been centered on socializing. If I attended an event, how many people would want to stand around and talk before I could get a seat? If I did find a seat, how much leg room would I have? Would it be possible to stand partway through the event if I needed to stretch? Would I be able to get an aisle seat so sitting and standing would be easy? If I really got in trouble with my pain, how close would I be to a place where I could lie down—and would there be ice? Of course not. Wishful thinking.

To ask for help had caused deep embarrassment. To use a cane, crutches, a walker, or a handicap parking sticker had invited questions and assumptions that had made me feel exposed and pitiful.

All the while, I would admonish myself. *Hey, Amy, it's not terminal cancer; it's just pain. Suck it up!* I was so stubborn I refused to identify as disabled. I hid my condition as much as possible. I was in serious denial, expecting too much of myself in an attempt to overcome shame at being an ineffective mother and wife. *Please, Lord, all I want is to be normal.*

So, about a week before I was scheduled to see my physical therapist again, and after the kids were off to school, I slowly and carefully made my way down the stairs. I tried to do some common tasks, like open the mail that had been piling up, organize some of the kids' school papers, and have a conversation with my folks.

But after sitting at the table and eating breakfast, I realized my energy was spent. I hadn't even been downstairs for an hour. I gingerly made my way back up to my room. After I got back in bed, I had to admit that even just a little bit of living normally had been exhausting. And this restarted all my doubts about the surgery and the pace of my recuperation. Why was I lagging?

The emotional roller coaster was about to begin. All aboard. All one of me. Crying was inevitable. Torrents of tears fell before I finally fell asleep.

When I woke up, I was not right. My body was shaking with chills one minute, and then the next minute I'd be sweating and nauseous. I'd watched enough celebrity rehab shows to realize what was happening. The bugs I felt crawling under my skin weren't there. It was my nervous system freaking out from my opiate withdrawal. *What did you expect, Amy?*

When the vomiting started, I stared at the pill bottle, thinking I could have one then and then slowly lower the dosage, like every doctor said you should. Or I could ride this out. Heck, it had to be almost over with, didn't it?

Ultimately, I abstained, and for the next twenty-four hours, I looked like any other junkie suffering withdrawal symptoms. It sucked big time. Although I'd taken the meds exactly as prescribed and had been slowly decreasing my dosage for a week before going cold turkey, I was learning that the body can remain addicted even though the mind is ready to do without.

In retrospect, I was darn lucky that nothing worse had happened to me after my rash decision to go cold turkey. Getting off opiates is like walking the plank on a pirate ship.

Except when you fall, you don't hit water; you hit concrete. Stupid, stupid, stupid. I'd suffered enough. A dumb, impatient decision had only added to my misery. Unfortunately, it would not be the last time that stubbornness and a deep craving for self-sufficiency would get me in trouble.

As I fell in and out of consciousness during my withdrawal, and lacerated myself for one more failure, I heard a voice in the back of my head. It was my PT counseling me before the surgery. He was offering perspective and compassion—and some tough love. "Amy, your recovery is going to be a slow year. A long, slow year."

*No. You're wrong*, I wanted to shout. I could get better faster. In six to eight weeks, I would be ready to tackle life again. My pelvis was stable!

Oh, if that really had been the only reason for pain, then that would have been true. However, I would learn over the coming months and years that persistent pain was much more layered than "just" bones and tissue.

Even during my dreary drug withdrawal, the absurdity of my wish wasn't lost on me. I couldn't even spend one full morning downstairs, and I could barely get up and down the stairs one step at a time while gripping the handrail for dear life.

Deep down I knew the voice in my head was right. It only meant more hardship, more months imprisoned in my bed.

"No, dammit!" I cried. "No!"

My spirits sank, dragged down by another voice, my own. *Will my body ever heal?*

# Part Two

"One day you will look back on this with all the wisdom time bestows and say…well that sucked!"

# Chapter 6

A new thought hit me as I anticipated returning to physical therapy. Maybe I was in a bad relationship—with my body and myself. How could I change it? My college days offered a clue.

The summer before my sophomore year at ISU, my body had appeared to be mending. I had regained some mobility, and the pain could be managed. So I had basically been normal with occasional pain flares that I had assumed had happened after an arbitrary movement that must have reinjured my ligaments. Yet figuring out what to do with my sexual urges had been another matter.

I had known I wasn't pure as the driven snow, the ideal others expected of Christian women. In high school I had had boyfriends, and we had explored each other's bodies and our burgeoning sexuality, though I had maintained my virginity. Only one boyfriend had gotten me to seriously consider giving up that prized status. The idea had so compelling, so appealing, and yet morally wrong that I had naturally sought the wisdom and counsel of my Young Life leader. Yes, that had been Jeff.

He had handled it well, as you would expect from someone more mature. Pounding the table and giving stern commands had not been his style. Instead, he had listened to how I felt and why I might want to "go further" with this young man. We had discussed Christ, the Bible, and the implications of sex before marriage. He had asked a pivotal question that I now see as egotistical and manipulative: "Amy, could you envision loving anyone more than this boyfriend? If so, maybe you should hold on to this gift and save it for *that* person." And who would that have been?

He had also engaged me in a talk about masturbation and assured me it was not a sin. Rather, it was a way of holding back on intercourse until that very special partner arrived. By the end of the conversation, he had convinced me to hold off having sex with my boyfriend.

Looking back, I realize that by confiding in him, I'd provided the signal he'd been waiting for. A virgin was there for the taking. She had confessed strong sexual urges. He wouldn't need to begin a conversation about sex. I had been ripe, easy prey.

And for those in that Christian environment who might have been appalled that we'd had an affair, something more important had been taken from me: trust. I had believed he had had my best interests at heart. When I had realized how foolish I had been, I had stopped trusting myself. For a time, I had believed I was incapable of making my own decisions or trusting my instincts. Years later I would regain that agency, yet it had harmed my interaction with medical professionals. Had I been a confident young woman, I'm sure I would have taken control of my destiny far sooner.

My call to Jeff near the end of my first year at ISU had been different, of course. I had been emotionally desolate. I had felt abandoned by my swim coach and the university. Although I had been making great progress in physical therapy—the range of pain had fluctuated, but I had been able to walk—I had had no idea what my future might bring, personally, academically, or professionally.

That summer, I had been nineteen years old. Had that made me a consenting adult, even though an illegal sexual relationship had begun a year earlier? Later, I would learn that sexual abuse comes in different flavors, and our relationship had been more like incest. There had certainly been something insidious about Jeff's approach. He had preyed on my beauty, wit, and naivete, as well as my wish to see the best in others. It had been wrong of him to approach and touch me.

And he had discouraged me from telling others about the affair by saying my hope of becoming a Young Life leader would be over. This had been his way of controlling me. He had known I couldn't take that risk; I hadn't wanted to lose my future in the organization. The manipulation had been subtle, yet the implication had been clear: an adulterous woman would not be fit for ministry.

Even though part of me had really liked being courted, had savored the sex, and hadn't feel like a victim, I had been fighting a war in my own head. Later I would learn the term that describes this condition: *cognitive dissonance*. Had the affair been damaging to me? Yes. But not damaging in the way others might think. This is why I think of it as more like incest. He had been a father figure to me. Once that bond had been breached, I believe the psychological damage had been far more profound than losing my virginity. As a Christian, I suppose I could justify loving the abuser while hating the abuse.

That summer before my college sophomore year, I had needed to be held and replenished. Life had beaten me down. Maybe expressing myself sexually would lead me to better days and moods. I had also discovered that while intercourse would not hurt my pelvis or increase my physical pain, it would hurt my heart.

Seeking out Jeff had not only been about sexual need or emotional support. From the start, Jeff and I would make love and then have deep theological discussions that had been engrossing and flattering to me. He had praised my grasp of complicated theology. According to Jeff, his wife had not cared to engage in these kinds of talks. Her faith, I had been told, had been simple, and she had wanted to keep it that way. She had wanted to love Christ, not have intellectual debates about his beliefs. I had also been told that she had been disinterested in the marital bed.

All of which had led me to a conclusion, reinforced by his manipulative narrative, that I had been a gift from God. I had been helping him be better, which is what I had wanted.

But even at that precious age, I had been aware that this belief had been ridiculous—that he had needed to do this just because his wife had been simple and hadn't wanted sex as much as he had.

By brushing aside the inner voice that knew right from wrong, I had convinced myself that it would be all right to enjoy sex with Jeff now and later date other men my age. In fact, he'd encouraged me to do as much, right up until that time when I had known I had needed to move on. That's when it had gotten scary. A conversation had begun that we would have on multiple occasions; it had made me feel responsible for keeping him alive even if I had been dying inside.

"I'll kill myself!" he had shouted.

"Don't say that."

"I can't live without you! I need you; you promised."

"Jeff, this isn't fair. Of course you can live without me."

"I need you to make me a better man. I can't be a better man without you."

I'd finally concluded that there was no way I could invest in a relationship with a man who had been cheating on his wife with a teenager. Had he encouraged me to see other men only to hide his other relationships? Stories would emerge. Dark stories. There had been other girls, and those relationships had been much darker and twisted than my experience.

Jeff's suicide threats had taunted me throughout my sophomore year. Not being a swimmer anymore had made me feel lost at sea. To replace the gap in my life, I had poured my passion for the pool into high school kids. I had used all that time and passion to volunteer as a Young Life leader. I had been stunned by the physical, mental, and sexual abuse many of them had endured. Where had all the goddamned, so-called adults who were supposed to care for these souls been? I had taken the kids into my heart, and to this day many of them have stayed in touch with me.

In fact, it had been my contact with these kids that had helped me detach from Jeff. I had told myself that I could not be an adulterer while knowing they believed that I had more answers about faith, God, and life than they did. By the end of the school year, I'd found a therapist. I had needed to tell someone every detail about the affair and its repercussions. She had been the first person who had suggested that what I had experienced hadn't been an affair but that I had been sexually abused. I had had no idea how to respond to that. I hadn't wanted it to be true. I had stayed at school that summer and taken my first apartment. My yearning for independence and the higher calling of helping others had given me the confidence I had needed to change my life.

Years later, marooned in bed, I needed to call on that success to help one more soul. Mine.

## RESTORATION REBOOT

Nearly three weeks after surgery, Tim came to the house for a friendly visit before the hard work started. I was soon reminded why we made a good team. His skills, experience, and calm personality were the perfect contrast to my Type A personality. Tim had an easy way about him that helped me relax. He was like my favorite sweatshirt that I would wear to bring me comfort. Worn, familiar, reassuring. He was never rushed and always had a smile on his face and a ready laugh.

The discharge from his care months before my surgery had been particularly rattling to me because I needed to bounce new ideas off someone I trusted. Tim always made time for me. After collecting information from websites and research papers, I would contact him with a barrage of questions. His insights had guided my choice of surgeon and hospital.

"Greetings," he said as he entered, all six feet plus of him.

At first our visit was a bit like show-and-tell at school. I demonstrated how I stood up from a seated position and then walked across the room so that he could assess my gait.

"Wow. I'm amazed how stable your walking is and how 'light' you look."

"Well, I have lost eight pounds since surgery," I said.

"No, I mean your expression, the look on your face. The stress isn't there."

Really?

Others had mentioned something similar, but I hadn't really known what they meant. I was still in too much pain, or just foggy from medications.

"And dang, when you're sitting or standing, you're not shifting positions every thirty seconds. Fantastic."

After the show, it was time for the tell. Sitting on the floor, we shared updates on our families and hobbies. Then I handed him the post-op program I had been provided after surgery.

"I'll read through it before your first appointment. Are you ready?"

I stared up at him from the floor, unsure of my own answer. "Yes?"

"Yeah, Amy, you're ready. Let's get back to work. You're going to be my Venus de Milo, remember?"

We laughed.

"Oh, almost forgot. Before I go…"

He handed me an envelope; then he was gone. I pulled out a get-well card signed by Tim and his wife. The caption read, "One day you will look back on this with all the wisdom time bestows and say…well that sucked!"

Made me chuckle, but there it was again—that annoyingly well-timed insightful thing he was so good at.

Fear and nerves accompanied me to my first appointment, but I was excited too. Now the real restorative work would begin. This time I didn't have to worry about an unstable SI joint. But the same old questions ate at me: Would Tim unearth more problems caused by the surgery? Was I in better or worse shape than I thought? My tummy was all tied in knots.

Since I was still not cleared to drive, Dad took me to my appointment. Tim greeted us as we came through the door, wearing khakis, a comfortably worn orange-and-blue plaid button-down, and his favorite brown-and-orange shoes, which made him look like he was about to start out on an adventure down a hiking trail.

Evaluation day—time to collect all the objective data on strength and all kinds of other boring things that would spell out the next portion of this journey and highlight all that was wrong so it could be fixed. I wondered why good news was rarely given on days like this. I knew today would include those SI provocation tests I had come to hate.

Many familiar tests followed. Since much of my rehab time had been spent on my stomach, where I couldn't observe Tim's facial expressions, I'd learned to read his tone of voice, pauses, and utterances. They all contained information. After conducting a bunch of tests, I could almost hear him smile. He was happy—giddy even. As I completed the motion he requested, his excitement could not be contained.

"Amy, your SI joint didn't move!"

I was elated. This was the reassurance I needed to know the instability was behind me (pun intended!). "I should hope not. They did put five screws in there!"

The rest of the data left a lot to be desired. I was weak everywhere, and we had only tested my lower half. In some cases, I had barely been able to perform the movements Tim had wanted. I felt so stiff and sore, and I had been afraid to move too much. These evaluation days had always flared me up and increased my pain, and I hadn't wanted that to happen again today. We made it to the end of his data gathering, and his face told me my discomfort wasn't as masked as I hoped.

"You still don't trust it, do you?" he said.

"I can't survive more setbacks, Tim."

"I get it."

"But I have to say, I'm trying to take a page out of your playbook and am feeling more hopeful than I have been in a long time. Fingers crossed."

Therapy with Tim usually included lots of variety. In the beginning, it would be very passive and very boring. Don't get me wrong. I loved a good massage and when he stretched me, but I liked the exercises best. I always wished for more of that. I figured I was too weak and fragile to handle them. Just being there felt like I was doing something to help myself, although most of the early days would be "damage control," as Tim called it. Passive treatments and machines and some baby exercises for me.

Toward the end of the session, all I was asked to do were simple heel slides. While lying on my back, Tim asked me to move the back of my heel up to my butt, but I couldn't do it. I needed a slide board, pillowcase, and a little assist from Tim to complete the movement. The new so-called simple exercises were frustrating. My muscles began to shake under the stress until my whole body was one big trembler. It was as if my brain and body were disconnected. It was embarrassing, humiliating, and ultimately demoralizing. *Oh my God, I really am a total mess. Here we go again.* I had been looking forward to this appointment and getting started on my rehab. But once again reality had proven cruel.

Tim showered me with encouragement and praise. "You're doing great. You're right where you need to be. Let's not get ahead of ourselves, all right?"

His professional insights took my internal crazy down a few notches. Thank God. I was beginning to think I'd soon need to be committed to a cell with padded walls.

"OK, time's almost up for today. Let's sum up. You're weak, uncoordinated, have a bunch of muscle imbalances, and are very guarded in your movements. No worries—lots to do, but we've got this. Over time that will change."

"Yeah?"

"Yup. And you won't always walk like a robot, I promise."

At that point, it was hard to imagine moving without thinking about it. It was so hard to believe that someday all this pain would end.

But in the days that followed, I began to look on the bright side. The infernal burning seemed to be gone, and I was finally sleeping, really sleeping, for eight hours without waking. That alone was an amazing gift.

After that first PT session, Dad took me out to lunch, though I was tired and a little voice in my head was saying, *Go home*. When we did make it back, I should have gone upstairs and rested, but I didn't, and that meant I'd been up and about from 8:30 a.m. to 3:00 p.m. Why did I push myself? I felt pressure to be making strides toward being "better."

Also, Dad's repetitive reminders of his hip surgery and assurances that I would "bounce right back" were not what I needed. Yes, I was improving, but very few people truly saw how bad my condition had gotten in recent years because I'd hide it by gritting my teeth and just handling the pain.

By the next morning, I was paying the price for my long day. My butt was on fire and incredibly tight, and spasms from my lower back all the way down to my knees made me panic. *I've ruined the surgery. Too much too fast. I've torn a muscle.* I fell into a deep dark place. It felt like I couldn't breathe, the pressure in my chest was so great.

Then another thought broke. None of this would be a surprise to a health professional. It's part of the game. I repeated the mantra endlessly to calm my nerves. *None of this is a surprise to a professional…*

The war raging in me was physical, spiritual, and psychological. On the one hand, my next-day pain was predictable. After several years of not being on my feet for more than thirty minutes at a time, I did not yet have the strength and stamina to be active for seven hours. Sheesh. Who knew, huh?

On the other hand, resting was hard. I couldn't believe the surgery had worked when, heck, I was still lying around about 95 percent of the time. The immobility made me frustrated and scared, even though it was for my own good, and Tim, Ben, and others had all urged me to rest and take it easy.

That's when I had my aha moment. It was riveting.

*Amy, you're not just recovering from surgery in the way your dad did. You're correcting eighteen years of stuff. Bounce back? No way, honey.*

Yeah, OK, that made sense. But I still didn't know if I could survive the emotional rodeo, riding high in the saddle, then being thrown to the ground with a searing pain in my ass. How in the world was I going to be able to balance all my own needs and the needs of my family?

Stop. Breathe. Believe.

Sanity returned. I took some Tylenol and reminded myself that I had meds left over from my postsurgery regimen. I promised myself that I would stay on top of everything and grant myself plenty of ice and rest. *Do just that much, Amy, and day by day life will get better.*

# Chapter 7

To any other family, my son Connor's swim meet would have been an opportunity to be supportive. For me, though, the event was bittersweet. It took place in a pool at the college I knew well. Although I'd gotten used to sitting in the stands, a lot of personal and family history was tied to the facility. Ben was a diving coach there. Both of our kids competed there. I coached high school swimmers there. And eighteen years ago, my body had gone to hell there.

Each visit tugged at my heart and knotted my stomach. I'd gotten pretty good at suppressing those feelings, but other times I could not help but wonder what might have been—in all aspects of my life—had I stayed healthy.

Regardless, four weeks after surgery, I could not bear the thought of not being there. Even though in past years sitting through the long meets on hard bleachers had meant days of recovery from the pain flares, on this night all I had to do was rest my butt on a padded red chair for three hours to watch my boy swim for less than three minutes. Despite the pain I felt every time a cheering able-bodied parent bumped me, I was all in. It was a joy to be there, to be present, to watch Connor express his love for the same sport I loved so much.

While the kids warmed up before the meet, a sea of bodies piling into the lanes, swimming together like a precision machine, I stared at the pool. I longed for the water like a long-lost lover. To swim, to be strong, to be free—the water begged me to leave my fears and concerns behind and dive in and fully submerse myself. I was a slave to its calling. I'd held on to that passion for years as I battled pain and physical dysfunction. And despite having been hurt, burned, and wrecked by a painful pelvis, still I could not resist the pull of the water, the clarity of mind I knew it would bring, the sensation of the water rushing over and past my body, the security of the lane lines holding me within their bounds, the knowledge that while competing I had had the power of mind and body to push myself farther and faster than I had thought possible.

Here's the kicker. When my physical therapist during my freshman year at college had told me to stay away from the pool, she had been taking away the one thing that had made me feel like me. She had been putting my ability to confidently move off-limits, which had furthered my belief that I was broken and fragile. Losing the ability to swim, coupled with my understanding of where my pain was coming from, had been the first step on a slippery slope of disability. I had been taught to fear the thing I loved and valued most, the place where I could surrender and be at peace.

So watching one more swim meet was a reminder that it had been too long since I'd given in to the wonders of the water. There were times I had all but given up hope of ever being able to swim again—really swim, with abandon, with body and soul, not just paddle back and forth. The dream of swimming again was all but dead, and then I met Winter. The dolphin, not the season.

In 2009, we spent Christmas in Tampa visiting family. A trip to the Clearwater Marine Aquarium introduced me to Winter, who would become the star of the *Dolphin Tale* movies.

As a baby, the bottlenose dolphin had been rescued from a crab trapline. The rope had wrapped around her tail and cut off the blood flow. After treatment at the aquarium, her tail had had to be amputated, which had meant she could not swim the way she had been meant to. Undeterred, Winter had begun moving side to side, like a fish. But when that motion had begun to harm her spine and create a muscle imbalance—similar to what I'd been told was the cause of my pain—she had received a prosthetic tail.

Her story won my heart. I was overcome with the hope that if this dolphin could adapt with the help of modern medicine, so could I.

When a whistle announced the start of another race, Connor stepped up on the blocks with the other boys and listened to the starter's commands.

"Swimmers, take your mark…"

The gun went off, and six nine-year-old boys exploded from the blocks.

And as quickly as it had started, the race was over. I smiled and gave my son two thumbs up as he grabbed his towel and went to his coach for the postrace chat.

My mind wandered as I stared at the black numeral 2 embedded in dingy gray tiles at the end of the lane. That spot was where my journey with pain had started. As though transported back in time, I could smell the chlorine burning in my nostrils that day while the fluorescent light flickered and the red and white lane lines blurred as I began my flip turn. Then the sound. The atrocious snap that had reverberated deep within me. Despite all the time that had passed, the memories of that sound turned my stomach. Then my little movie, in full Technicolor, replayed again:

CLOSE-UP *of my feet hitting the wall for a standard turn I've done a million times before, but this time—snap!*

THE VOICE IN MY HEAD. *What was that?*

*From the edge of the pool, hands grab for me and unceremoniously pull me out of the pool by my hips and flop me on the deck. I lie on the cold tile of the deck, crying, afraid, and so alone. Part of me dies on the deck that day. I have just sustained a life-altering injury that will take months to diagnosis and decades to fix.*

CLOSE-UP *of me laid out on the cold surface, crying, afraid, and alone.*

THE END.

Cheers brought me back to the swim meet. By that time, I'd been sitting for a couple hours and feeling OK. For the first time, I thought my injury hadn't beaten me. It hadn't stolen my life. I hadn't drowned or died on the wet tile. *No, Amy, you are reclaiming your life. You have help from family, friends, and medical professionals. Tim has even said he will figure out how to get you back in the water!*

I needed to hang on to all those hopeful thoughts. I needed to believe that I just might be able to live the rest of my life without the excruciating, all-consuming pain I had known for so long.

Physical therapy followed later that week. As Tim worked my soft tissue, we began a conversation much like the others we had shared during my treatment. They'd wander and include laughs and revelations. Maybe that was because it was easier for me to talk while lying down and not having to focus so hard on simple things, like remaining upright and breathing.

Then Tim asked a question that brought tears to my eyes.

"Amy, how are you doing with the emotional side of your recovery?"

It caught me off guard because no one else had ever asked. Mostly, people would ask how I was doing physically. Then we'd veer into my modest accomplishments, setbacks, responses to treatments, etc.

The question opened a floodgate. It was an invitation to express the crazy things that were running through my mind.

"I'm afraid, mostly, that I'll never get free of pain and live a normal life. My hopes and fears change so fast. One minute I'm high from an hour of moving well, then suddenly I'm in the dumps."

I also told him about the feelings that had been aroused at Connor's swim meet. I wasn't weeping, but

I'd have to pause now and then, to choke back tears. Tim responded to my silences with, "I'm still listening."

I decided to believe him and kept talking. There were no judgments or expectations there. By then I trusted Tim enough to know that he was giving me permission to speak honestly. The safety of that conversational space was priceless.

When I finished talking, he looked me in the eye and smiled. "I am confident that we will have you back in the water, even doing flip turns, just down the road from here. There is much to look forward to, Amy."

I smiled too. Then he increased the difficulty of my exercises, and I had no doubt I would hurt the following morning.

But so what? I refused to be knocked down emotionally by tough moments in my recovery. It felt like a whole new world was opening to me. A world of possibilities, not limitations. A world of endless pain-free days.

In the following couple of weeks, physical therapy grew increasingly harder, and each session wiped me out. Afterward, I was in desperate need of a nap. Yet the sessions were the highlight of each week. They were ruled by the same values I adhered to while training to be a competitive swimmer: no pain, no gain.

Tim was patient with my zillion questions. The interrogations were my way of pinpointing my pain. Only then could I learn about my body, the musculature, the way it worked or failed. With each exercise I'd ask, "What's this?"

While he plied my soft tissue or put me through an exercise regime, I'd ask, "Why does that hurt" or "What makes this exercise so hard?" or "Ouch. Tell me the name of that muscle?"

We went from simple table exercises to things a bit more involved, where I had to move body parts and not just tighten a muscle while lying on a flat surface. I experienced a split feeling of simultaneous accomplishment and failure. We were taking on more challenges, yet when I couldn't do ten repetitions of an exercise, my heart would sink.

"What?" Tim asked.

"I really despise that these simple exercises are so challenging for me."

"It's opportunity for improvement, that's all," he said with a smile.

His remarks diluted my disappointment a little. But then we moved on to "dog points." While on all fours, I tried to lift my right arm and left leg at the same time. Nope. It was like my leg and arm didn't understand my command. I despised that feeling.

"Don't get down on yourself. It's an opportunity for—"

"Why won't my body do what I ask it to do? Just pick up the right arm and left leg—just a little—but *nooo*. My brain and muscles don't seem to talk to each other."

My frustration in those moments grew because usually, with other exercises, Tim would praise my effort, and then we'd move on to something else. But this time that didn't happen. Instead, he wanted me to work on lifting arms first and then legs separately at home. Then we would try it again next time. Next time. I wanted it then!

My annoyance cooled a bit when we analyzed the progress toward our therapy goals. Stairs. Getting easier—check. Walking fifteen minutes without increased pain—check. Sitting thirty minutes without increase in pain—check. Swimming—not so much, but maybe soon.

My life was not only about me in the physical therapy treatment room. At night in our bedroom, Ben and I would talk about the kids and my progress. Although my body was improving—he noticed, and that was enormously supportive—there was another hurdle to overcome.

"Ben, it's hard to be so isolated."

"Maybe you should spend time with friends. Focus on your hobbies and that kind of thing."

"But after PT, I have zero energy. And I still don't trust my body, so I don't feel safe caring for the kids."

"Just take care of yourself for now. Connor and Erin understand," he said.

"But that's what torments me. It's normal for them not to see me much. I hate that."

"That will change."

When he repeated that I should reconnect with friends, the people who cared about me and understood my limitations, I groaned, but he was right. Despite my fatigue, I needed to take my fight to another battlefield. By going out, I would begin to face that big old world out there as well as my fears about lifting my feet over curbs and not finding easy places to sit. It was not only a matter of building my physical stamina. My emotional well-being also needed work.

"You're right. Thanks, Ben."

He smiled, then turned off the bedside lamp. In darkness I made a commitment to let friends take me away from my home and reignite my interest in simple pleasures, such as saltwater coral reef tanks. Just thinking about the brilliant colors lifted my spirits. A week later, another kind of excitement made my heart soar.

Tim and I went through our usual routine, including the exercises that had been so challenging. Then he stopped and said something I didn't expect to hear for a long time.

"Amy, I think it's time for you to get back in the water."

My heart began to pound. The suggestion thrilled my inner child, as if she'd just been given a pony.

"Swim, you mean? You're letting me swim?"

It was obvious what he was saying, but I needed clarification. I wanted to be sure I hadn't just imagined what he'd said.

"Yes, but under two conditions. One: your feet can't touch the walls of the pool. Don't get ambitious and suddenly decide to try a flip turn. Two: no more than ten minutes in the water. Again, I don't want you overdoing it and hurting yourself."

From there we discussed nitty-gritty details, such as how I would get in and out of the water and who would assist me and make sure I respected the time limit.

"You have to be smart and safe, Amy."

It felt a little like my overly protective father laying down the law before I headed out on my first date.

"OK, OK, I get it. I'll be careful. I'll go slow. I will pay attention to my body and not overdo it. And I will not stay in past my ten minutes and turn into a pumpkin."

My whole body smiled. I was going to swim again. I couldn't wait to tell Ben. As a diving coach, he had keys to the ISU college pools.

It only took one telephone call to get permission to swim in my old haunts. We packed up the family and headed off to play in the water.

Once we were in the facility, Connor and Erin sped off and dove in, splashing around while I made my way to the edge of the pool. My joy was replaced by fear. The dimensions of the pool felt daunting. Memories also began to hammer me. I was terrified of getting in.

Gingerly, I sat on the edge of the pool, embarrassed by the tears that flooded my eyes, thinking to myself, *I can't do this. I can't get into the pool.*

It was as if I were confronting my abuser. My love affair with swimming had done me harm. The sport and facility I had loved with rare abandon had become an enemy to be feared and resisted.

Ben stooped close by. "Amy, you OK?"

I nodded.

"Just follow the plan you and Tim made. Do what Tim told you to do."

Ben was right again. My PT and I had talked this through.

Get in the water by the ladder, one rung at a time.

Swim.

Get out by the ladder.

"Need help?" Ben asked.

I shook my head and reminded myself that I wasn't a slowpoke or moron. I hadn't forgotten how to enter a pool.

I started down the ladder. The water felt cool against my body. Fear was still close, but I kept it at bay with logic and reason.

Once I was submerged, I did something I am ashamed to admit. Too afraid to swim with long strokes, I began to dog-paddle. If my teammates could have seen me. A former college swimmer doing the doggy paddle. I didn't know if I should laugh or cry.

It felt so good to be *in* the water. Its embrace calmed and reassured me. This was home. This was where I had thrived and given as much as I received. True love.

When my kids saw me attempt to swim, they cheered. Their voices echoed throughout the tiled facility as I made it to the edge of the pool and pushed off with my hands to head back to the other side. After paddling around for a few minutes, I got a little braver and started swimming normally, with my legs gliding behind me, until I decided to try a kick. To my genuine surprise, nothing fell apart or fell off or went snap, and I felt wonderful! Why hadn't anyone had me do this sooner? I could feel a flame begin to flicker, rekindling the deepest reaches of my soul.

When my time was up, Ben helped me up the ladder and wrapped me in a towel. I sat poolside watching the kids play until I had recovered from my exertion and could get up and get dressed for the trip back home.

That night I slept soundly. I'm pretty sure I was smiling.

# Chapter 8

The first big test of my new physical abilities came one morning when I heard Erin crying out for me at the bottom of the stairs. It was a hideous, pitiful, 911-emergency kind of cry that enflamed the primal mother instinct in me. I flew out of bed and bolted downstairs. It wasn't until I hit the bottom step and scooped up my daughter that my brain caught up with my body.

*Hey, you just ran down the stairs!*

*That was kind of cool!*

*Yeah. Do you have any idea how long it has been since you* ran *anywhere?*

Then the doubt and fear I was so practiced at hit.

*You know you will pay for this later, right?*

I cleared my head and asked Erin what was wrong. She sobbed.

"Honey, *what*?"

"My Nemo!"

"What?"

She pointed, so I hobbled through the living room to discover that her saltwater fish tank had sustained a death. And it was grisly. Sea cucumbers are marine animals with leathery skin and long bodies. They look like large turds and are super fun to watch—especially if you are in grade school. Unfortunately, they are also very much like an atomic bomb. When they die, they explode and take out whatever is around it. All her fish were floating at the top of the tank, including her favorite little clown fish. Since I was the only one in the house with the knowledge to help her with the tanks, she had screamed for me when she had seen the disaster.

"Oh, sweetie."

"Why?" Erin said. She needed an answer. How many times had I expressed the same anguish but for different reasons?

I let her cry and gnash her teeth, and we cuddled. Mama and her baby girl. Tons of cuddling, and then she pulled herself together and went off to school.

"Bye, Mama."

*Mama.* My most prized title. Also a job that I felt I had failed at the most because of my pain. To feel in that catastrophe that I was needed and could rise to the occasion lifted my spirits. Maybe I was more able than I really thought I was. Or maybe I had just wrecked my surgery and set my healing back by weeks or months.

At my next PT appointment, it did not surprise me that Tim noticed something was different. Upon the start of the soft tissue work, he asked, "Um, Amy, what did we do to get like this?"

He was referring to the hot, swollen, and tight tissue that hurt to be touched. I explained my dash downstairs.

"Aim, I suggest you set aside your marathon training plans for now and next time just walk down the stairs."

"Even if the house is on fire?"

I promised to smother any urge to run again—ever, and we both laughed. I hated running, so it was an easy promise.

But I would do it in a heartbeat if I heard Erin or Connor call out "Mama!"

## A BRIDGE TO SOMEWHERE

The following session with Tim would prove to be a big deal, a milestone, even though I had my worries when he announced our next step.

"Today we get to start bridges!" he said.

Tears welled in the corners of my eyes. My stomach knotted with anxiety. One more time I had to risk telling Tim about the deeper thoughts in my head.

"I'm scared." To say it out loud was a relief and embarrassing. I was a grown woman afraid to perform a movement because of the way it always felt. Meaning, it would hurt. I couldn't take any more pain from trying to get better. It would crush me. My resilience was small. I needed more wins like the ones we had been having and couldn't handle failure again.

Tenderness filled his eyes and was expressed through his touch and tone of voice. My embarrassment washed away, and I was glad I had shared my fear. The raw truth had enabled my clinician to respond with compassion. His response made me feel safe, heard, and supported.

"Hey, hey, hey, it's OK. I wouldn't ask you to do something I thought you couldn't

handle, Aim. You're ready. I'm right here. Nothing bad is going to happen. Let's just start with one, OK?"

It may not sound like much to lie on your back, bend your knees, and then lift your butt off the floor or treatment table. But this simple exercise had caused me great amounts of pain prior to surgery. I had faithfully stayed with a bridge regimen in hopes of acquiring buns of steel, and all I had gotten were buns of molten lava.

I lay on my back, and he stood beside the table, guarding me with his hands, ready to help if I couldn't do it, which now seemed ridiculous. I mean, really, what was going to happen? I did this same type of movement in bed all the time without even thinking about it. But somehow, while at PT, this exercise represented a special form of torture.

I performed a full bridge, slowly up and then slowly down. After that successful first attempt, all the worry that had built up rushed out of my body, and I completed the remaining nine without fears and tears or pain.

These small victories would slowly pile up and help improve my outlook. I was starting to do things I had never done. They felt different. I was in a state of mind that was quite different from my mind-set before surgery. By giving myself permission to talk about my fear, we were making progress. If I could do the same exercise that had destroyed me in previous years, that was a good indicator that we were headed in the right direction.

The prior week had been good too, when we had added single-legged standing. I had had to work hard to remain upright on one leg. It had forced me to concentrate so hard my face had turned purple and I hadn't been able to carry on a conversation, which Tim had found amusing. Usually, I was chatty and would ask all kinds of questions. But his teasing always part of the care. When I had finished, he had wanted to know how I had been doing.

"Did that cause pain? Are you still doing OK?"

Often, I would have to think about it to give an honest and accurate assessment. Polite autopilot answers wouldn't help. I was glad he asked for feedback because it gave me a chance to say I was not OK or report new sensations. During this session I had given him a puzzling answer. "You know, I'm not sure I know what not fine feels like. Yeah, I know that may sound crazy, but I've hurt for so long that I often can't tell the difference between fine and not fine."

Tim's response had been revealing. "Aim, anything causing increased pain while you are doing it is *not* fine." Then he had caught himself. "But wait, you usually don't feel it until later, do you?"

It was true. I could make it through every entire PT session, and although they could be challenging, it was the kind of challenge I could live with. I would keep at it as long as a limb wasn't going to fall off and I was sure the exercises would help correct whatever was causing my pain.

On the other hand, continuing to work with my "no pain, no gain" philosophy might not have been very helpful. I'd always looked at PT like training, the same as when I had been a swimmer. Getting stronger wasn't always comfortable. Stronger meant breaking down muscle so that it would rebuild and become stronger.

Tim's comments had made me question my perspective on pain and what was acceptable and what wasn't. "You're right about the process of strengthening a muscle. We do have to break it down. But it's a normal process and it heals quickly. The body is really pretty amazing when you think about it, Aim. Discomfort caused by therapy should last no more than a few hours. I would like us to avoid pain. If you find you are in more pain after treatment, we need to adjust."

So I would be the gatekeeper, so to speak. If my pain and discomfort increased or lasted more than twenty-four to forty-eight hours, I would need to tell Tim so that we could adjust. The insight had grounded me. I had then had a better way to qualify what I was experiencing. By being more discerning, I could no longer lump all pain into one category. And it had given me a better means of communicating more accurately with Tim about what I was experiencing.

After the bridges, we finished with a round of soft tissue massage that launched another one of the conversations that had become such an important part of my journey.

"I know my piriformis is angry at me," I said. "That darn muscle has been angry since way before surgery, and everything I do seems to set it off—sitting, climbing stairs, walking, possibly even breathing."

Tim raised an eyebrow.

"Well, OK, not breathing, but it feels like anything sets it off. The pain triggers so quickly and intensely and without warning that I can go from fine to not fine in a heartbeat. And sometimes it's sneaky. Everything seems fine until I lay down and then *bam*, it feels like it's trying to choke my butt!"

"Aim, we have to remember that eighteen years of pain and dysfunction will take time to undo. Remember our deal? I get at least one month to work toward recovery for each year of pain. I expect that these aches and pains, and the tightness, will continue to be moving targets as we continue through your recovery. They are just muscle imbalances that will eventually end. Nothing we can't handle."

When he put it that way, it seemed like a fair explanation. In retrospect, talking about tissue sensitivity versus damage would have been much more helpful to me in understanding why everything and nothing could set off my pain.

## AFTERSHOCKS

Despite all the new insights, the morning after my physical therapy, I felt like someone had beaten me below my waist. Adding the new exercises had been challenging, but I really didn't expect that I would feel like I had been run over by a truck. It frustrated me. This was exactly what Tim and I had talked about. Did my body really need to wait twelve hours before reporting its displeasure? The delayed responses were doing a number on my head. You thought you could do these things, but maybe you couldn't, Amy! How could such small exercises create so much pain!

At the end of the week, my parents insisted on taking me out to dinner to my favorite Japanese restaurant.

Dad said, "We want to celebrate the successful surgery and that you're getting better and no longer need our help."

It was true that we were all sensing the end of their time with us. But even as I agreed, my sixth sense told me that it was a mistake. I didn't think that I could sit for a long meal without experiencing pain, and my PT session had already caused a flare-up.

But my parents had been so helpful and encouraging. Dinner out was their way of expressing their love for me. I felt I owed it to them to wear my "I'm not in pain" mask one more time, even though it went against my PT's advice. These are the compromises we make, sometimes not wisely. Why couldn't I just say no? I knew it was more than I could handle, but it was like I had to prove something—what was I trying to prove? That I was getting better, that I was going to be OK?

The trip required that I walk downstairs again, get into and out of the car, and then enter the restaurant. My emotional and physical strength was waning as I sat on a chair that was hard and uncomfortable. We hadn't even ordered yet, and I was already exhausted.

I thought, *Why am I here? This is dumb. I should have said no.* It didn't matter that someone else thought that by now I should be able to go out for a family dinner.

Those thoughts set off my guilt and shame. *What is the big deal? All you have to do is sit here and enjoy your favorite meal at one of your favorite restaurants. Think positive. Just be happy; be thankful. Count your blessings.*

The truth was, I was tired of feeling like a disappointment to everyone.

I sat quietly and tried to enjoy my favorite food, but my butt was in knots, which made it feel as though I was sitting on hot rocks. As much as I tried to smile and talk with my parents, most of my energy was needed to search for a comfortable sitting position and to hold myself upright. My whole being was exhausted.

Finally, I gave up and tried standing up, walking to the bathroom to stretch. I was beyond caring what anyone, including the other diners, thought. I needed some relief and couldn't sit for one more nanosecond. The pain was invading all parts of my body and overwhelming my attempts at positive thinking. I was angry that I was there, and my parents didn't seem to understand how hard it was for me. How could they be so oblivious?

Despite the frustration, I was paralyzed with self-consciousness. Everybody else in the restaurant was able to sit and eat. Yet I squirmed and grimaced and couldn't even make breezy small talk.

Then a voice intervened.

"I'm taking Amy home."

Ben had been watching me and had realized I was in agony. This was unusual for us. Usually, we would discuss these situations and make decisions together. I was enormously grateful that he had decided to take charge. Relief washed over me.

I don't recall any protests or more talk. Ben walked me to the car and we headed home. After climbing the stairs to our bedroom, Ben massaged the hot spots, but everything was on fire.

Sometimes we're just not capable of taking care of ourselves, even when we know the right thing to do. We become lost in a sea of our own expectations. Those are the times when the term *caregiver* takes on profound meaning. Someone with a compassionate heart needs to intervene. Someone else needs to advocate. On that night, Ben had risen to the occasion and given me the right to set limits without regret. It was another unexpected lesson learned on the path to recovery and independence.

# Chapter 9

The changing of the guard was another milestone. After weeks of assistance, my parents left the building, and Jess, my BFF, arrived to take their place. The most important people in my life had come to my aid. My gratitude ran deep.

Jess and I had become fast friends nine years before after we had moved to Maryland to be closer to Ben's family. When circumstances, jobs, etc. had demanded that we return to Normal, Illinois, leaving Jess had been like amputating my right arm. Although we scheduled visits twice every year, the time together was no substitute for the way we had shared our lives when we had lived in the same place. We had missed our most recent January visit because of my surgery, and that had made me angry. Our previous visits had included long drives to Alabama, where the kids and I would play for a week. Our kids were the same age, and all got along beautifully. This allowed Jess and I to spend the week scrapbooking and catching up on all the things sisters catch up on. No, we weren't actually related, but she was like the sister I had never had, and the kids were growing up together like cousins. The trips had been a challenge to my body, but I had dealt with the pain because I got so much from spending time with Jess.

Since my postsurgery condition had made travel impossible, Jess came to me and provided around-the-clock support and encouragement. Despite my joy at seeing her, I was horribly embarrassed that I needed so much help. And yet she knew and loved me so well; I did not need to hide the darkest, ugliest parts of me because I knew her dark places too. Our friendship was, and still is, unconditional.

Before my surgery, we had shared a weekend together that had allowed Jess to probe every nuance of my discomfort. She had been desperate to understand how it felt to live in my body. Every hour she had asked me to describe what I was feeling. Frankly, it had been hard for me to constantly describe how the aches burned, stabbed, and made me feel raw and tight, as though someone were cutting into me with a hot knife. "It's like someone stuck a screwdriver in my backside and is trying to pry that joint open," I'd said.

"What?"

"Everything feels out of place. Or I feel like fire ants are living in the depths of my tissue, biting me all day and night."

"Oh my God! How can you stand it?"

Unfortunately, my descriptions hadn't provided any relief for me. And her questions hadn't ended when we had finally gone to bed at the end of the long day.

"How does it feel now?" she'd asked, hoping that her earnestness had somehow lowered my pain.

I had wanted to lie but couldn't. "The same. It always feels the same."

A tear had rolled down her cheek. "I'm sorry, Aim."

Jess's curiosity had been admirable. I'd never intentionally hidden my pain, but looking back I know that I also didn't talk about it much unless I was with a doctor or physical therapist. I felt it was my responsibility to push through it, this thing that was as much a part of me as my four limbs and my heart and mind. Only Tim knew the real story because he saw me at my worst. Therapy was the only place I was emotionally raw and honest about how hard it was.

So the week Jess was with me, I decided she deserved to be let in, all the way in. The best way to do that was to invite her to my physical therapy appointment, where I was at my most vulnerable. The data, so to speak, would be raw emotion, because from the very start I had believed Tim would not be able to help me if I didn't express myself—bluntly at times. I'd complain about the difficulty of doing common things, like getting out of the car and walking into a grocery store or sitting through a movie. I'd also blurt out how I loved watching my kids swim but hated sitting through swim meets. It was the safest environment I had ever been in. I was completely accepted there, all of me, exactly as I was. PT was the only place where I didn't try to suck it up and pretend I didn't feel like a complete failure and burden to my family. Tim always accepted my confessions, declarations, and questions without judgment. Often he did so with amusement and even keen interest. It made me feel safe. Jess would finally get to see what I had tried to describe; I had always been vulnerable with her, but this was different somehow. Showing her my emotional vulnerability had never been an issue, but my physical weakness, that was something else entirely, and it was all going to be on display. I was afraid she would no longer see me as her capable friend and would maybe even want to label me as disabled.

Tim was wonderful, as always, talking with her as he worked on me, chatting about everything and nothing. They both took the liberty to tease me about my quirks, which they both knew so well. It made me smile and forget the rawness of my body.

When we moved into the exercises, the conversation flowed easily. I enjoyed the support and interaction, until…

I had barely started the standing exercises when fatigue lowered the boom. There was no hiding the breakdown, my jelly legs, the struggle to remain erect. Tim and I exchanged a look, which was a complete conversation with no words. He understood how important it was for me to let Jess see what real life was like, but he also empathized with how my weakness often caused me shame. He was asking if we should continue and expose my exhaustion or call it quits. Finally, I spoke. "It's OK. She's my rock."

He smiled. "I thought I was your rock."

"No. You are the sculptor otherwise known as Tim who promised to restore Venus."

Tim didn't skip a beat. He told me to start my next exercise. I took a deep breath and started. My balance was off; it was difficult to simply stand on one leg, much less deal with the motion caused by the activity of my other swinging leg. Forget Venus. I was the Leaning Tower of Pisa. I faltered.

I heard Jess let out a small gasp and knew she was suddenly, totally inside my world. My weakness was horribly obvious. I struggled like a chubby toddler trying to take her first steps. Before I tumbled on my face, Tim intervened, and we moved on to a different exercise until it was time for the stretching and massaging.

Later, Jess would tell me that my struggle had been hard to watch. "I hated to see how hard you have to fight to get your life back. But, Aim, it was the best thing you could have done. Thank you."

Now that's true acceptance and a friend that is closer than a sister.

## SPRING BREAK

When Jess returned to Maryland and Tim departed for a much-deserved vacation, I felt a big hole in my world that was more than filled by my kids on spring break. More than two months since my surgery, it was the first time we were home alone together. I had conflicting emotions: I was excited to take on more and manage my life, and I was totally terrified that I might tumble into a world of hurt for trying.

Recognizing limitations was helpful because I'd learned with Tim that trying to do too much too fast only increased my pain and slowed me down, which mentally destroyed me. Pacing was a difficult concept for me, but I was starting to learn how to balance my up- and downtime. But it was spring break, and I was supposed to be making memories with my kiddos. I did the best I could to play games and do crafts, run an errand, and maybe hit the drive-through for lunch. I mean, come on, we all know Disney World would have been so much better. I just hoped that the kids would have fond memories of times together and not remember how painful and hard everything still seemed to be for me.

But wasn't I getting better? On the one hand, I could not complain as much about the pain when, clearly, it was less than it had been before surgery. On the other hand, my discomfort was still ever present, and it could get pretty bad. I did not want to live forever in a semirecovered state. PT was slowly restoring my physical self-sufficiency with what felt like endless self-care routines that were meant to help me avoid the horrible burning sensations that had burdened me through the years.

Yet another anxiety haunted me. I knew that someday fairly soon, I would be discharged from physical therapy and would need to be able to take care of myself. It was difficult to imagine being in full control of my own care and management, because let's face it, there was still pain to manage. Those damn muscle imbalances, when would those be gone? When would I be strong enough not to hurt? And why did these imbalances cause this much pain? Lord knew it wasn't an unstable pelvis anymore; that had been taken care of in surgery. But when would my body be balanced enough to stop hurting? It felt like an endless war. I was winning some battles, but I wasn't sure I was winning the war.

While Tim was away, I made a few appointments with a massage therapist to work on my lower body to keep things loose. It felt great. If only I could have afforded the treatment once a day. It was dawning on me that my recovery would demand a lot more than just Tim and me. The most important person on the team was me. I was the one responsible for following the course of treatment that had been lain out for me. I vowed to keep after it.

In moments of doubt, for months and years to come, I would get back on course by recalling a fifteen-minute walk I took that spring break with Connor, who was ten years old at the time. On a cold but invigorating day, as we circled our block, I was all too aware of the intense concentration it took me to walk the way I had been instructed. The effort needed to walk "correctly" was immense. I had been taught to consciously tighten my stomach muscles and glutes, making sure to fire those glutes at the right time. I had been told they didn't function like they were supposed to, at the right time or in the right way. My favorite term for this was *dumb butt syndrome*, or *lazy glutes*, or *gluteal inhibition*. All of those felt true. After learning about these muscle imbalances and my dumb butt syndrome, it seemed amazing that anyone could walk at all.

Then Connor chirped, "Mom, you're walking really fast these days."

His comment touched me so much I could have crushed him in my loving arms. And he was right. Despite my concerted effort, there was progress since my surgery. My legs were swinging much more freely. I didn't have to drag them anymore.

The next day Erin took a turn walking with me. It was important for me to see my progress through the eyes of others, especially my children, as they always had a way of putting things in perspective. They sure didn't think my butt was dumb. They thought I was pretty amazing. I realized if I could see myself as they did, it might do me good.

## MILES BEFORE I REST

Tim's return from vacation excited me, even though it meant we were going to up my exercises, and that probably meant I'd be plenty sore afterward. Before we began the workout, Tim gave me a symbolic pat on the head for being prudent, a good girl, and not overdoing it with my kids over spring break. I was learning to embrace the small victories in my journey. They may have seemed slight at first, but if they could improve my mood and lift my spirit—even for a day—I was grateful.

Tim and I were aware that though we had long passed the six-week post-op protocol, I was still in pain, and it made this journey feel endless. I now had had sacroiliac joint dysfunction, or lower back pain, ligament damage—call it what you will—for half my life. I had to stop myself from imagining what I might have accomplished with all that time if not for my ailments and setbacks.

On spring break I'd complimented myself for developing some strength in my abdominals and glutes. But I soon realized it wasn't enough. I fought like hell to do five lousy reps of the latest in Tim's restoration routine. God, it was hard. Tim said, "Good," but part of me wanted to scream.

The two-steps-forward-one-step-back rhythm was another dimension of the treacherous mind game. *Give me more. I'm ready. I'm a competitor.* Then I would get exactly what I asked for and feel like a failure because, well, it was harder. It demanded another level of mastery, another level of endurance and skill. With each growth spurt, I predictably hit a wall when more muscle power, coordination, or endurance was needed.

At home I found myself trying to outsmart the burn that Tim's tough workout would likely cause. Should I take Tylenol to ward it off? Before my surgery I'd gotten used to ignoring pain and just letting my body hurt so that I wouldn't further injure myself. That was crazy. I wondered how in the world I ever could have thought that. But I had. Sometimes I wondered how in the world an eighteen-year-old wound could have never completely healed. Was there a different way to explain all the pain I had felt through the years? If so, wouldn't someone have told me?

Do you see what I mean about the mind game? It never ended because it was multilayered. Physical and mental habits became ingrained and ruled the day. Then I wanted to improve my situation, but that meant disobeying thoughts that had in the past seemed helpful.

That evening after therapy, I decided to take an over-the-counter product and not read too much into it. I couldn't let a couple of aspirin define my recovery, could I? Of course not, and the decision helped me realized that my mind was feeling better. The brain fog was lifting. I was able to think more clearly and beyond the moment to anticipate what might be waiting around the bend. This meant I could focus for longer periods, and that gave me more confidence in the long game. The endless pain had made it difficult to see past the day's agony. But as Tim's restoration began to take hold of my body, my head started to wake up from my coma of pain so that I could do what I'd once truly enjoyed—study, learn, and solve life's problems. My incremental improvements had made me realize how much I'd missed those things.

In fact, the liberation allowed me to begin dreaming about how I might help other medical professionals and patients better understand SI joint dysfunction and lower back pain. New seeds were being planted that foreshadowed where all this misery might lead me. Educating others by finding answers for these types of problems thrilled me. The wish to contribute began to shape my prayers. *Let me help other women and men so they didn't have to give away half a lifetime.*

Not that I didn't include me, myself, and I in my prayerful moments. I still had miles to go before I was out of the woods. Yet even to consider expanding my horizons and taking on more responsibility was telling. A mere ten weeks before, I had been terrified that my life would always be broken and I'd never move out of the clutches of "I can't."

I praised God, my family, friends, and my thoughtful PT for the progress. And before laying my head down for what I hoped would be a good night's sleep, I quietly promised that I would someday help others overcome fear of the unknown. It should not be so hard to find help for these kinds of problems. I knew I was not the only Venus buried in the rubble. Others were out there also desperately wanting their lives back.

# Chapter 10

There is always something bigger than personal pain and circumstances. We are not always entirely aware of the events and people who shape us or the motivations and beliefs that drive our behaviors. Other powers and people shape us with their talents and love. A concert about three months after my surgery reminded me that there was more to my past than debilitating pain.

One of my most favorite people ever was coming into town. Andy, a former Young Life kid of mine, was coming home to fulfill an old promise to me. He was coming home to perform a concert to benefit the current high school kids in our local Young Life group. Andy and I had remained in touch.

It had been an amazing thing to watch him grow from a member of a little high school band called the Normals into a musician signed by a music company. When the band had broken up, I had been sad. But the breakup had given way to new opportunities for the members. Andy would go on to produce his own music and that of others and spend time in the group Caedmon's Call.

I knew there had been dark times for him, but it had always thrilled me to watch God provide for this talented young man as he told deep truths through story in his music. I would listen to his albums over and over, as if they were prayers to God. I knew this little concert would be a holy moment, attended by people from a good span of my life, and I wouldn't miss it for anything.

To this day, some of my fondest memories are of Andy and his best friend, Mark Lockett, playing guitar and singing in my living room. They had been amazing together. When they had played, it had been like Heaven itself had opened and blessed us with the sounds they had made in their effortless harmonies. They had joked that when they became rich and famous they would return to Normal to help raise money for the local ministry. That's how grateful they had been for the experiences they had had during their time with me and the ministry.

Nothing in my college years had been better than being with those two boys and their friends. If I had helped them through those years, the opposite had also been true: they had helped me see something bigger than the loss of what was really a very small NCAA athletic dream. They had helped me start to see a bigger picture, outside the persona of the swimmer, outside the self-critical labels of a harlot who enjoyed sex with an older married man, outside of someone broken by pain. These kids had represented a new, beautiful, vibrant Amy. They hadn't seen all the brokenness I had seen. They had seen someone who loved them fiercely. Who believed they could do anything. They had met a woman who made them question and think and learn to understand themselves and scripture. They had shown me I was the safe place they had needed to be real, to let down their guard, to ask hard questions, and to wrestle with real answers. This very special group of kids had shown me just how much I had had to give of myself, when I hadn't thought there was much worth giving. By serving them, I had found myself.

Nearly fifteen years later, Andy was a seasoned musical veteran who still shared his love of people and God through song. The concert funds would help send more kids to a week of summer camp at one of Young Life's many beautiful properties.

In a sense, Andy's return was a homecoming for me too. After Ben and I had moved our family back to Normal from Maryland, I had volunteered to help with leadership training and loved it. My time and talents had been put to good use, and I had been fulfilling a purpose and passion in my life. The role had been excellent because, years after having worked with Andy and others, it had allowed me to teach, one of my great loves, and express my passion for helping high school kids find their voice while discovering themselves and their thoughts about Jesus.

Getting involved with the group again had eased the isolation and intense back pain I had experienced after returning from Maryland, where I had left the dearest friends I had ever made. When I had been given the opportunity to teach and share my experiences from my time on staff and in the ministry, my suffering had lessened. My pain had become more tolerable. I had had a purpose.

Yet before Andy announced his concert, I had resigned from my volunteering. The physical pain had been too unpredictable, which had forced me to miss meetings, and I hated being unreliable. Also, all the stress had been causing disruptions in my marriage. Ben and I had grown distant and unhappy.

For all those reasons, showing up at the concert and reuniting with my tribe was an occasion I could not and would not miss.

When we arrived at the church where the concert would be performed, it was about 5:00 p.m. Excited Young Life leaders swarmed me with hugs, and I was reminded how much I missed the connection to them and the ministry. Here I was being showered with love, and yet I felt so unworthy after having resigned my post.

It wasn't long before the "kids" I had mentored started trickling in. Joy and a mama-like pride filled my heart to see them all grown up with families of their own, living such satisfying lives and still actively involved in their faith. It was joyous and humbling.

We gathered plastic chairs around a table, and everyone began sharing stories about YL moments that had impacted their lives. Tears gently rolled off my cheeks as they shared story after story of how my being there had made a difference. I loved them more than I could ever explain. They probably did not know how profoundly they had changed me. They'd taught me so much simply by allowing me into their lives. As a result, I was a better person.

They all wanted to know about me and my family and how we were all doing. Before I could answer, one of the leaders, named Kelly, distracted me by whispering in my ear. "Andy just told us that you were his Young Life leader. We want you to introduce him before the show. We can't think of anyone better, so just say yes, OK?"

For a moment, my mind raced with what I might say. The majority of people in the audience were his high school friends. They didn't need me to recite his resume. And those that didn't know him probably didn't care about those details. I decided I'd better just speak from the heart.

I went to the front of the room, took the mic, and looked at everyone seated around tables and standing in the back of the room. "I feel honored to introduce my friend and your friend. He's going to tell us some wonderful stories about life, love, and Jesus…in song…"

My soul warmed to the moment. I was surrounded by friends, people that cared about me, loved the same things I did, and still wanted to learn and grow in their faith. The sense of connection and appreciation and anticipation of Andy's performance was huge. My heart was so full, fuller than it had been in a long, long time.

At some point during the performance, I paused and wondered if I had been ignoring some of the more subtle signals my body had been sending because I was enjoying myself so much or if there had not been anything to sense. When I stopped to check in with myself, I could sense maybe it was time to leave, like I had negotiated with myself earlier. How could I leave these people, this beautiful evening, when I felt so richly and deeply blessed?

## BODY SPENT

By 11:00 p.m., I was still at the concert, and my body was screaming. *We had a deal; you were going to listen to me this time. You weren't going to wait until I was screaming at you to listen. You broke our pacing agreement!* I chose my default coping option and told the voice to shut up. I was in charge, and we were not done yet. I was staying.

When the concert ended, I lingered to chat, and once again I was rewarded with kind comments about our time together through Young Life. Then as the audience began to leave the church basement, reality hit me like a cold blast of wind. How was I going to get out? I wasn't going to let Ben carry me.

I stood, accessed my options, and sought a solution. The stairs seemed to be the only way out, so I devised my plan. I leaned against the wall, gripped the handrail, and pulled myself up the stairs one slow and painful step at a time. It felt like lead weights had been added to my pelvis and legs.

Outside I shuffled forward with small steps, gingerly inching my way to the car, one hand on the wall of the building to steady myself. Without that support, I was sure I would have fallen. I was struck, once again, by how much change could happen in the way I moved and felt after something as simple as sitting. I knew this was normal for where I was in my recovery journey. In past months, I might have thought I'd done more damage or something was terribly wrong. But that wasn't the case.

I was in pain for good reasons, but those reasons weren't all physical. I was beginning to see that my moods and thoughts had something to do with flare-ups.

Once we were home, I carefully maneuvered to get out of the car, then held on to Ben for dear life. As soon as I lay down in bed, I wondered how much damage I had done. I reviewed how hard it had been to get up the stairs, how heavy everything felt, the burning sensations, the way my walk had worsened. All those things indicated damage, right? It had been wrong to sit there for so long. I had overdone it. My mind raced again in a stupid whirlwind of doubt and frustration.

Ben brought me ice packs.

"I wonder if I should call for a PT appointment in the morning."

"I don't know. Wait and see?" he said.

Within thirty minutes, the burn had backed off, yet my butt muscles were frozen and numb from icing. Maybe I hadn't done anything wrong, and I was going to be OK. Either way, things were calm enough that I drifted off to sleep.

By morning, most of my lower body felt sluggish and swollen. And though my pain and movement had improved, I was still not back to my new level of normal.

One moment I was fine, taking stock, and the next minute I was alone in the house, where I'd lain facedown on my bedroom floor. I started to cry and couldn't stop. It felt as though something inside me had been dislodged, and I could no longer hold back a tidal wave of emotion. A sense of loss—deep, aching, soul-wrenching loss—shook my body.

There was so much I wanted to accomplish, so much I wanted to give and share, and yet despite my best efforts, I was still broken, damaged, and so fragile that I could not even enjoy a night out with people I loved and who loved me. How could they be so thankful when all I had to give was 5 percent of my being? Why would they love somebody like me? No, they didn't love me; they loved who I had once been, and I didn't know how to give like that anymore because I felt like my pain held me back.

Despite recent gains, I was losing the ongoing war between my internal processing of pain and true external events. I couldn't bear the contrast, for example, of those sweet kids I had poured myself into years before with where I was now. Inconsistent, unable, and disabled. The thought scorched me. I had never used the word *disabled* to describe my status before, but it was really what I'd become. They had prospered and matured, whereas I had floundered and failed. I felt like a deflated beach ball. Unlovable and no good to anyone anymore. It was killing me. There was so much passion and life inside me, and I was totally unable to find a way to let it out. Andy's concert and the reunion with my flock had only intensified my longing to be able to give of myself 100 percent, just as the new Young Life leaders were so generously giving.

The emotional breakdown revealed that I had no perspective. Even measurable improvements working with Tim were meaningless as I bawled my eyes out on my bedroom floor. I was not an inchworm, goddamn it. I wanted to soar. Yet I could not even sit and listen and be with the people I loved without suffering disabling pain. That realization scorched my heart like a red-hot sword. I was breathless as the life I might have lived, its breadth and depth, flashed before me, feeling forever out of reach.

While bearing the burden of disappointment and unworthiness, I felt trapped in a foul, stagnant weather front. The fog of despair engulfed me. It felt like a funeral. My funeral. I was in mourning because I believed nothing would change, that I would never have the body I required to match my heart and passion for life.

I shouted and cursed, prayed, and cursed some more. I was exhausted by the difficulty of my journey and the desperate grab for hope. The thought of having more work ahead of me was unbearable. Couldn't we skip to the other side? Couldn't I just blink and have the hard road be traveled? I would then be done with this!

Then the darkness broke for a moment. My mind, soggy and morbid one moment, had suddenly cleared. *Amy, you have a choice.*

Do I whine and wait five more days until my next PT appointment?

Or do I call now and ask for help, help with managing not just the bodily breakdown but the mental anguish?

The Young Life kids, my protégés, my teachers, came flooding back at me, filling my heart and mind with reminders. All those years ago they had needed help. Their lives hadn't been perfect. They had joined a community that could provide guidance and sustenance. I was among the people they'd looked up to.

*Amy, you can't do this alone. In fact, you're not expected to do this alone.*

What a mess I was. I hated calling in when it was not my scheduled appointment, even when I was desperate for attention. I feared I was sucking up more than my fair share of care. I didn't like being a burden. Yet the clinic staff had always been wonderful to me.

*Amy, you're the one who is making this harder than it needs to be. Speak up. Ask for an extra helping of hands-on, ever-loving care. You deserve it. You need it. You are worth it.*

I won't suggest that it was easy. I will not pretend my gut didn't ache with anxiety as I dialed the phone. For a moment I just ignored the tsunami of thoughts in my head and pretended I was *normal*. Fake it till you make it, right? A normal person wouldn't hesitate to call.

When the receptionist put me on hold, I had to listen to bland background music. This stuff sucks, I thought. They should play Andy's songs.

*Andy.*

His sweet melodies streamed through my mind, the deep truths convicting me and binding up my hurts all at the same time:

> *We were so sure we'd change the world*
> *And I need my Jesus now*
> *But I've been angry for the longest time*
> *And I just don't know how to let it go*

Because we were so sure
We would change the world…

*Apron full of stains,*
I wanna give You everything
But I've got nothing of my own at all
And if I give what I have not got
Will You fill me up and make me whole…

*The best I can*
And this all feels the same
But you've brought me to this place
Where there's nothing else but faith
And this is what I have been given
And I will make the best I can
There's a joy we find in living
And a love that's in Your hand

"May I help you?" The receptionist was back. And I was singing.

Late that day, Tim went to work. He threw everything at me: stim, ultrasound with bio freeze, massage, stretching, and more stretching. It was fantastic. Then he pulled out the kinesiology tape. I was a little embarrassed by how much skin I needed to reveal so that Tim could tape me up, but the relief I felt was worth the blushing.

I was unusually quiet throughout the session. My emotions from earlier in the day were still raw. I couldn't make small talk, so I let Tim work, until he asked, "You're quiet. What's wrong?"

A funny thing happened when he asked me questions. His concern always seemed so honest that I hated answering with anything less than the whole truth. This thought, though, I couldn't find the words for. I was still trying to figure it out myself. Something to do with loss and disability and the way I viewed myself versus reality. It was all a jumble in my head. I just knew nothing was how I wanted it to be.

My favorite lyrics rushed into my head: "This is what I have been given and I will make the best I can. There's a joy we find in living." It was way past time to start living like life had joy again. It was possible that my life seemed so hard because I had lost my joy. I had stopped living. Coming to understand and accept that would be healing. Learning to find joy again would be pivotal to getting my life back.

# Chapter 11

Swimming continued to be a miracle drug for my body and soul. In the pool, again, I felt stronger, more so than I had felt in years. I even let myself push off from the wall with my feet. Not a flip turn, mind you. I kept my promise to Tim not to get too aggressive. Way in the back of my mind, I did wonder why he thought doing a flip turn would be too much. In some ways it seemed strange to be encouraged to push toward all those exercises I didn't like in PT but at the same time limit me in the one thing I truly enjoyed. I assumed there must be a good reason he thought it was so dangerous.

Even so, to push off rather than stop, turn around, and begin swimming was satisfying. I limited my workout to six hundred yards and felt like a wet noodle when I tried to climb the ladder out of the pool. I was glad Ben was there with me. I needed him to help stretch out the muscles in my hips and butt.

My expanding strength and endurance also allowed me to handle more normal household chores: a load of laundry here, a rack of kitchen dishes there, picking up after the tornado that was my kids. I felt pretty darn good when I did just one task, rested, did another, rested, and so on. Learning to pace myself was one of the more challenging portions of my recovery. The days where I mixed up sitting, reclining, and taking action seemed to be the better days.

Despite improvements, I continued to be annoyed with the burning sensations in my rear end. The burning thwarted my efforts to do the things I wanted and needed. I wanted to plant a garden with Erin after clearing out all the dead stuff from the previous fall. I also needed to create a scrapbook for a friend, plan Connor's birthday party—a real one with games and kids and cake and a theme. I also wished that I could hide Easter eggs for the kids to find on the holiday weekend. Nothing too grand, and yet some tasks were still too much to handle since they also required shopping and set-up on the big day. One task begat another.

And then there was my impulse to volunteer for Young Life again to be supportive of others. And there were my gathering thoughts about launching my mission to speak about the back pain and joint issues I had experienced. I refused to let my pain only be a bad memory. It was a repository, really—an encyclopedia of experience to be shared.

Yet nothing was ever fast enough for me, even when change occurred.

For instance, walking on uneven ground had been very painful before the surgery, even just to walk in my own yard. Four months after returning home from the hospital, I was walking on a sidewalk when I noticed a kid on a bike speeding toward me. Rather than freeze on the concrete, I stepped onto the front lawn of a neighbor to avoid a collision and realized there was no pain. It made me smile and take note. That was different!

That experience was a revelation. I realized that I would be able to go to the Fourth of July fireworks in my hometown that year. And I wouldn't have to medicate before activities in fear of painful repercussions.

This new phase of improved strength and mobility was not all rosy. To my friends I confessed that my expanding abilities scared me a little. I didn't always know what to do with myself as I entered a stage of recovery that I welcomed yet couldn't help but doubt. It was like dipping a toe into the pool to test the temperature. Was it safe to dive in?

The possibility of a future where I could do whatever I wanted felt like a mirage. I feared that the closer I got to seizing it, the quicker it would fade. Feeling a little better was a far cry from ultimate control. My journey was a day-to-day tactical challenge that was far from over, and yet… the idea that this could end someday was like a taste of something fresh and delicious.

There were other matters to consider too. I'd lost seven pounds after the surgery but since then had gained them back and then some. The extra weight made me frustrated. I felt like there were so many things to address to find the joy in living. In a moment of sanity, I decided the weight wasn't something I needed to focus on. There were ways to handle it and not feel like I was failing. Instead, I would treat it like postpregnancy weight and pretend I had just given birth to a new body. Since the extra pounds hadn't appeared overnight, they wouldn't disappear fast either.

Privately, I had to admit that my eating habits had been less than stellar. I often craved (and caved into) sweets and carbs and lots of coffee, even when water would have been better. Not to mention skipping breakfast, which had only added to the dietary chaos.

In truth, I had no system, no rhythm for life anymore. I'd cared for my body but now needed to give some loving care to ideas about living a full life.

## GOD IS GOOD

On Easter weekend, I joined a small study group that focused on God's goodness. The discussion began by watching a video that asked, "What is the most difficult thing in your life right now? What singular thing would you ask God to fix to make your life better?"

You're kidding, right? How could He not know?

I didn't mean to make a scene in the middle of my living room, but it was like God had spoken directly to me in that moment. He had heard me and was now ready to answer my prayers. The tears began to fall—a heavy rain that was a mix of gratitude and frustration. Where had He been? Why had He taken so long?

That sounds sacrilegious. Please understand, I was thrilled that God had helped. But I would be remiss to pretend that my patience had not been crushed more times than I could remember. I had been horribly broken for a long time before the answer came.

I stopped sobbing long enough to hear the next part of the video narration: "God's goodness doesn't always match what we think is good. But He has provided you with the kindest answer possible to bring this about…"

*Really? OK. I guess.*

Although still a bit skeptical, I began to count the small things that could bring about what I believed would eventually be my complete recovery. For now, the best possible means included the gift of my small group, the compassion of my PT, and the many people I had connected with since I'd begun posting on Facebook.

My takeaway from the lesson that night was clear: we can't and don't always understand God's ways. I am not sure I will ever understand suffering this side of Heaven. I did know that God took horrible experiences and transformed them if we let Him. I found comfort that night realizing I could help others by sharing my years of suffering, pain, and loneliness. I had always believed that when we shared our stories, we inspired others to make it to the other side.

The revelation got me thinking about the holiday we were celebrating.

Good Friday is good because resurrection cannot happen without death. That resonated with me more than ever that year. My passions, gifts, and talents, which had been buried by crippling pain, were being redeemed as I was resurrected in the healing process. Venus had been found and was being restored. I imagined the soil being carefully removed, layers of grime rubbed away. That's how I felt. Like the layers were slowly washing away. I was excited by what I was discovering.

On Easter Sunday I woke up feeling weak on my left side from the waist down. I chose to ignore it and see if it would go away.

I attended church for the first time since my surgery, and the entire celebration was lovely. Although I was not feeling as strong as I had for the last few days, it was wonderful to sit through the whole service without unbearable discomfort. (But while others stood at the start of the service, I opted to sit and sing my heart out.)

Afterward, at home, despite the uplifting morning, it felt as if the muscles wouldn't or couldn't do their job. So for once in my life, I accepted it. I was learning to accept what I could and couldn't do in any given moment. I was learning to accept today. To accept this moment. It was a radical change in my understanding of pain that would be pivotal in my recovery. Learning to understand the difference between "I can't right now" and "I can't" became a lifeline. I was learning to stop fighting myself and my own expectations and just be. I spent my day of resting in bed with the TENS unit.

As my weary body and mind unwound, I wondered if I was being too cautious. That was a far cry from my previous fears of pushing too far.

A day or so later, I woke up with sinus drainage and a sore throat. I was delighted. I could handle this. A little sore throat had finally won my attention. Fantastic. I couldn't remember the last time I had considered the common cold *painful*.

Change. It can be found hiding in the smallest places.

## CUDDLING WITH A SAGE

Change would also be demanded of my husband and children, though I didn't realize how big that might be until one night when I cuddled with my favorite ten-year-old, Connor.

This was a routine we both had enjoyed before my physical problems had gotten so bad that I had had to get in bed by 4:00 p.m., when Ben got home from work. Connor and Erin would come in to say good night because it was too painful for me to bend over and give them a kiss before limping upstairs.

When I crawled in with Connor, we naturally started talking about all kinds of stuff, some of which was silly and funny. After some time had passed, my boy looked at me and said, "Mom, you better get back to your room. I don't want you to hurt more."

"It's OK, honey. I can do this now, and it doesn't hurt."

"I can see you're getting better. You do the stairs more; you walk the dog. And you are downstairs with us more and not always in your room."

"Uh-huh. Anything else?"

"You laugh more and don't look so sad all the time."

The sadness that he and Erin must have seen in me so often was sobering.

"And you haven't fallen down once since the surgery. Well, OK, you dropped that pot lid on your foot yesterday, but that didn't scare me."

That my immobility had scared my kids made my tear ducts fill up. "It used to scare you?"

"Yeah, you'd fall down, and my tummy would get all tight, and then you'd be in so much pain. I'm glad that doesn't happen anymore."

"Me too."

"I think you used to look so sad or angry sometimes because you wanted to do more with us and you couldn't."

"That's right. It did make me angry. It wasn't fair. I wanted to be a better mom." The emotion made my voice warble, so I shut up.

"It's OK. We love you, Mom."

Wisdom and reassurance from the mouths of babes.

I hugged him tight and thanked him for loving me as I was and reminded him that there was a lot more to come.

"I'll keep getting better, and we'll do more and more."

He nodded. My ten-year-old sage. Then he started talking about Harry Potter and Legos.

The real impact of our talk hit me after I'd tucked him in and gone back to my bedroom. I was so hard on myself for all the things I felt I couldn't provide. But overall, the conversation left me hopeful. Hopeful that my pain hadn't ruined my children. That they didn't see me the way I saw me. They didn't see me as lacking.

Yet Connor's awareness of my emotional state was shocking. His father had never seemed to notice, and yet this tender child had seen the emotions I thought I had hidden from him. As my boy continued to grow and mature, it would become more and more evident this conversation was a testament to his empathy for others, which he credits to growing up with a mom in pain. Years later, he would still remember my body giving way in the kitchen as one of the more helpless feelings he had ever experienced. I hated that he had experienced that, but I am glad I was wrong about the way my children viewed me. While all I saw was what I couldn't do, they saw all that I did do. What a fantastic perspective.

## THE PAIN GAME

When the body is in a constant state of hyperarousal, also known as fight or flight, it sends out cortisol and a variety of other hormones and neurotransmitters. They work together to protect us from threat. In my recovery, I sometimes felt in withdrawal from all that. Clearly, my body wasn't feeling as much threat as it used to. Yet I still felt defensive and hyperalert to emotional and physical pain.

For example, I often felt the urge to pick a fight with Ben or the kids. I just wanted to be mad at someone; even the dog would do. It was as if something inside me was saying, "You need to stay mad and keep fighting." No, I didn't. But I also wasn't used to living without all those chemicals constantly rushing through my body. The need to pick fights reminded me of other stressful times in my life.

Past counseling had helped me understand that my body was used to responding in certain ways and I would need to unlearn those habits. By doing so, I would eventually find a new level of normal.

I wondered if this was how top-notch athletes felt when it was time to retire. Did they miss the competition so much that they needed to find other ways to vent or express the battle instincts? My years fighting to heal my body were as long, or longer than, most professional sports careers. Maybe I wasn't ready to retire from the long-term emotional, mental, and physical crises. When I coupled that with other types of emotional traumas I'd experienced, I concluded that the need to fight might have been part of who I had become. Understanding there were chemical changes happening within me as my threat level changed made it easier to forgive my random emotional outbursts by accepting them as part of the process toward healing and wholeness.

It was all about perspective. I had to mourn the losses the severe pain had brought to my life. My body felt like it had been through a war. And while I was eager for a cease-fire, regulating everything was a little like negotiating with a gang of rebels who refused to come out of their hiding place and lay down their arms.

# Chapter 12

I now owned the label: I am a sexual abuse survivor. But it took me a long time to get my head and heart wrapped around that concept.

The change began to take hold when I was a senior at college on the verge of graduation. One night while I lay in my waterbed, about to doze off, the phone rang. It was Jeff. I sat up when I heard his voice. Something was wrong. His voice was so different, my stomach clenched. "Aim, we need to talk."

The lie I'd been telling myself, that I was special, that I was having an affair with a married man who adored me, was crushed with a few simple words.

"My wife caught me with my hand on Rita."

Rita was a friend of mine and a little younger. I was outraged that Jeff would take advantage of her. Only for a fleeting second was I aware that I should be feeling those same things for the eighteen-year-old named Amy who'd been seduced by her mentor.

"Amy, if the police call you—"

"Police?"

"There are other complaints."

"You mean other girls!"

"You have to keep our affair secret or—"

"No! I'm not going to lie for you anymore."

My voice had turned steely with a man I had once adored. *You told me I was precious and special, dude. That's broken now. Any allegiance I might have felt for you is gone.*

Jeff continued to plead for mercy, but in this moment he was no longer the suave seducer. He was a pitiful, desperate man. In my sophomore year, when I had wanted to break away from him, he'd threatened suicide. On this call I was so unsympathetic he must have known he had to switch tactics to keep me quiet. If I didn't keep our relationship a secret, he would ruin my reputation in the Young Life community. I'd never get another job in the ministry. My family would disown me.

These were troubling taunts. By then, I knew I wanted to teach and be on Young Life staff to share my faith and life with high school kids. I'd lost my dream of competing at the NCAA swimming championships and leaving my name on the college record board. I'd replaced that passion with my devotion to God. Jeff knew quite well that he was jeopardizing not only life as I knew it but my future.

As we fought, I felt a tidal wave of grief and regret. That first kiss on the beach years before had been wrong. Right then and there I should have said no. But he had been a skilled manipulator. After a kiss on the mouth or "accidentally" grazing my breasts, he would apologize and pretend to be profoundly ashamed. He had feigned the sinful, fallen man who could not control his urge to *know* me so that I would be sympathetic. This is how predators work.

Despite my fear of the shame and consequences of exposure, I reminded myself, *Don't kid yourself; there must be other girls.* There were, but in Jeff's mind that was all *my* fault.

When he knew I wasn't buying his nonsense about loving me, he asked, "What's your favorite ice cream?"

Was he out of his mind? What did that have to do with anything? He pushed, so I blurted out, "Pralines and cream."

"Yeah, that's a special flavor, Aim. Like you. You're pralines and cream. All the others were vanilla. I could never replace you."

Excuse the expression, but sweet *Jesus*. Really? A special flavor? No. More like flavor of the month.

As difficult as the phone call was, at least it completely changed my perspective. By the end, I hadn't wavered. "You're not my lover who needs my protection. You're a predator. You deserve to be exposed."

The case against Jeff would state that he'd fondled four other female minors but had stopped short of having sex with them. The court would find him guilty of "abuse" and "assault," the appropriate legal terms for the crimes. Why wouldn't I be on the list of "victims" presented by the prosecution? Statute of limitations. But there would still be plenty of evidence to send him to prison.

My conversation with Jeff may have lasted eight minutes or eight hours. I don't know. I was lost in space, in another world. The entire event bent my mind and time. When we finally ended the call, I was emotionally rung out. I had no idea if my roommate had heard portions of the argument. But if anybody had been listening, he or she likely would have been startled by my cry of anguish at the very start. No! What a fool I'd been to think that I was his one true love.

I pondered what my next step should be. Clarity came quickly. I was afraid Jeff would get away with his abusive behavior. I picked up my phone.

The first call was to my boss at Young Life. She was a toughie, and our relationship had not been ideal. But she listened and then immediately acted by suspending Jeff from his volunteer position in the ministry and scheduling me for counseling. To this day I remember the moment when the therapist said, "Amy, I think you need to accept this was a sexually abusive event."

Next, I called the pastor at the church Jeff worked for. He was enormously supportive. The community leaders handled it right. They believed me. I did not have to suffer the disbelief and doubt so many other women had faced in similar situations.

My final call that night was to the police department where the claims against Jeff had been filed. I told them everything.

After the phone calls, I curled into the fetal position and cried all weekend. I let it all out, knowing that on Monday I would have to face a class full of fifth graders. I was finishing my student teaching requirement and did not know how I would be able to stand before them with a smile. It was not just my broken heart that I feared would thwart me. The pain in my backside suddenly flared and was astronomical, off the charts. I'd never been under so much stress.

Years later, during a return trip to Georgia to meet with my surgical team, my understanding of pain would evolve dramatically. I would begin to see pain as a warning signal to the body. A warning of what?

Danger, emotional or otherwise.

I had not been in pain before Jeff had called that night. A couple years had passed since the physical therapy sessions I'd had in Chicago, and I'd been doing well. But at the time, I did not make the connection between extreme emotional stress and my body. Instead, I blamed all the pain on my dutiful fitness workouts. To keep my core strong, I was devoted to Jane Fonda and *Buns of Steel* videos. I assumed that sticking to my regime, fearful of a relapse, was the reason for the burning pain I endured.

On Monday, with lower back pain I could barely endure, I made it through my teaching assignments. I was not so sure I would be as lucky when I faced my fiancé to tell him that I had been screwing my mentor. Ben and I had become engaged after meeting at school and Young Life events. Our dating had been free of stress. He hadn't pushed me into bed or made sexual overtures. At the time, his courtesy had been reassuring. I could not know then that his reluctance would be a foreshadowing of troubles to come. In any case, I was sure my world would collapse as soon as I made my confession about Jeff. Fortunately, he was supportive and stood by me.

The therapy sessions Young Life set up helped me navigate the emotional typhoon I was experiencing. To enhance my treatment, my boss also sent me to a retreat designed for women who had been sexually abused by clergy. I was shocked at the number of women who had also been abused by people in this powerful position. In some cases, there was still pain from events that had happened over forty years before.

It wasn't a good match. I fought some of the language that was used. When I was told I was a victim of abuse, I insisted on describing myself as a survivor. I've taken the same stand ever since. The v word didn't and doesn't sit well with me. The event was completely wrong and totally his responsibility, due to his age and position of power. That was easy for all to see. There was another portion that was slightly harder to accept and difficult for some to hear. The scars of sexual abuse come in different forms for different people. I felt some responsibility for choices I had made while the abuse was happening. I had to hold myself accountable.

In fact, what damaged me most had not been the sex. It had been the abuse of trust, the lies Jeff had told, and the lies I had told myself. That trauma would stay with me for years. It made me doubt myself even after I had accepted that the affair had never been about forbidden love.

At the retreat, I didn't dare admit that I had liked the sex. How could I say that the sensuality had been an awakening and therefore fulfilling? The admission felt twisted, like a sin, even though it expressed something fundamental about my identity as a woman. It would take many more conversations with skilled therapists to untangle the emotions, meanings, and events surrounding my sexual identity. In many ways it was no different than understanding those same things around my pain. Doing the work to untangle both stories would eventually lead to health and healing.

# Chapter 13

On a whim, after a challenging physical therapy session that had left me shaking like a leaf, I stopped at a thrift store and discovered brand-new practice swimsuits. Score! At retail stores these one-piece suits usually cost about seventy-five dollars. I was delighted to pay only four.

On the drive home, I realized that these little bubbles of joy—even just shopping for bargains—sometimes lulled me into thinking I was very close to being done with my physical challenges. Although the surgery seemed like a lifetime ago and it had only been four months, I knew I still had many miles to go before I could say, "Restoration complete."

As time wore on, I found that it was getting harder to tell friends and acquaintances how I was doing. They all had their own opinions about where I should be at this point. For example, one day I went outside to get the mail, and a neighbor I have known for eighteen years looked at me and said, "So why aren't you better yet? You had surgery a million years ago."

What could I say? The adage "Time heals all wounds" never measures the hours and effort needed. I just looked at the man I considered a friend, smiled, and said, "Yeah, it was a million years ago, but they told me it would take two million to recover."

He hadn't meant to sound critical. He just wanted me to be better. Even so, it was getting hard for me to respond to the inquiries. I just wanted to *be* without having to explain where I was in the restoration process. Sometimes my answers made me feel a little guilty, especially when I said I was good but admitted that I still had lots of work to do before I'd be great. Many well-intended people see health as a straight path, the luxury of never having had to heal. Nope. Not for Venus, nor anyone healing from trauma. I'd have good days followed by bad days. I began to realize that many people really didn't want to know the truth; they didn't want to hear that I still was not 100 percent. I couldn't blame them. Very few people, including medical professionals, really want to hear anything that isn't positive. There is so much nuance to the simple question, "How are you?" Well, which part of me are you asking about? I hated disappointing people by not being completely well for them. There were times that I wanted to lie so I could melt the friendly questions and the tension they caused me into thin air. On the other hand, I didn't want to lie or cover up the truth of what I was experiencing.

## GIRL'S NIGHT

My level of recovery was put to the test when my friend Emma invited me to her home to hang out with the girls.

"Come on over."

"Well…"

"Aim, we're just going to sit around and talk our heads off. And *drink*. How hard can that be?"

Emma picked me up at my house at 6:30 p.m. and would not return until after midnight. Despite the full evening, I would not need pain pills, Tylenol, tons of ice, or my TENS machine. It was wonderful to be able to focus on my friends without worry.

Catching up made me feel like Rip Van Winkle, the villager who fell asleep under a tree and woke up years later. One of my friends arrived carrying a five-month-old baby with her. I thought, *Oh my God. I don't remember even knowing she was pregnant.* It was a stark reminder of how long it had been since I'd socialized with my tribe.

I was enjoying myself so much I was surprised when Ben called—at about 10:00 p.m. He asked if I needed him to drive me home. Frankly, I was annoyed. Here I was working hard to find my independence again, and my hubby calls. I told him, "Emma brought me here, and she will drive me home—when I'm ready."

Maybe it was rude of me, because Ben was only trying to show his concern. He too had been on high alert for years. But I hated when his concern made me feel fragile. Too often I had felt held back by his worry and concerns. I was unable to articulate it at the time, but now I can see that this dynamic between us encouraged me to be dependent.

Fortunately, the evening did me no harm. In fact, it did me a lot of good in ways I wasn't expecting.

Connor's birthday was coming up, and I mentioned that I was worried about all the setup and cooking I needed to do. I could handle the party itself, but how would I mow the lawn and clean up my house? The girls, in chorus, responded.

"Why didn't you ask us for help?"

"Uh…" It was difficult for me to admit that I felt ashamed about my pain and so didn't reach out. But I finally spilled everything, and I was rewarded for my honesty.

"You've been hiding how hard it's been?" Emma asked.

"Well, yeah."

"That's dumb," somebody said. And everybody agreed, including me. Duh. I felt so much better when my gang took over.

We quickly divided the tasks into groups—indoors and outdoors.

As each friend volunteer for a task, I felt a terrible burden lift from my shoulders. Why hadn't I done this sooner? (We already know the answer.)

Some girls helped clean up the house, and they were wonderful, even though I was unusually specific about how I wanted things done for the party. The main floor needed to be mopped, and the butterbeer and other goodies were not going to make themselves.

One friend spent forty-five minutes picking up the back yard; another came with her husband and three kids. Together they blitzed the house, inside and out, and even revved up the weedwacker. Ninety minutes later—presto!—everything was glistening. After the big shebang, they also cleaned up so that I could lie down and rest.

But here's the kicker. They all thanked me for telling them exactly what I wanted done so they could be of help and feel useful. Honesty really is the best policy.

## 95 GOING ON 36

One of Tim's patients paid us a compliment after a tough session that had included steadying myself on a balance board while holding onto a TheraBand that he had pulled in all directions.

"That gal is going to need surgery if you're not careful with her, Tim," she said.

We laughed, and Tim explained that the rigor of the exercise was just the right level of challenge for me, if I paid attention to him!

I cherished the moment because it was more proof that I was hugely improved.

Ruth and her husband, Al, who had suffered a stroke ten years before, had noticed my progress because their appointment was right after mine.

"You know, Amy, when we first met, you looked a lot like Al after his stroke," she said.

That comment hit me hard. She was right. A few weeks into my therapy, I was struggling with the same exercises as her husband. God bless him, but it had taken Al years to get there, and now I was blowing past his milestones. It was a harsh but helpful look at reality. Right after surgery, when it had been time to get started again with Tim, I had been terribly uncoordinated, deconditioned, and afraid. My legs had felt like they weighed a million pounds, and breathing during the workout was hard. I had looked awful, like maybe I was ninety-five years old. Now I was feeling more like a 36-year-old mom.

And my mind was all pepped up with new thoughts. *Maybe I should get on a bike or try jogging.* What? Trying a 5K race would go against my absolute hatred of running. I was a swimmer. I lived for the glide, not pounding concrete, blacktop, or park paths.

I also considered popping one of my yoga videos into my DVR. Or maybe I could explore scuba diving again. *And what would happen if I tried to walk a mile and a half today?* In other words, the world was opening. I was ready for new challenges.

Not that I was pain free. My butt still hurt, but less than the previous week. Bending was still a challenge. So I was sure there would be more sudden reversals, and I'd find myself crawling to bed to calm things down. Even so, I had ambitions for getting outside and working in my garden over the Mother's Day weekend, like a normal person.

Normal doesn't always mean serene. I enjoyed hanging around with Erin and Connor and enjoying the simple things, like sitting on the porch reading a book in the sun while the kids played. I'd occasionally toss a ball to them or settle an argument. Mom duties. It was a big deal for me not to be isolated from my family and propped up with pillows and ice packs in my upstairs bedroom. I even got a little sunburned, but that's when the ruckus began.

Ben came outside and saw how red I was. "Aim, you've got to go inside now."

Once again, he was only trying to be helpful. This was his way of showing concern, I told myself. Yet my internal reaction was to yell. *Why would you send me inside and separate me from our kids? I don't care if I burn to a crisp, as long as I am here!*

Fortunately, I stuffed those comments. They seemed a silly way to respond to someone who was trying to protect me. But I wanted him to have the confidence in me that Tim did. I wanted him to see me like the couple at physical therapy that thought I was doing so well. To appease him, my compromise was to move inside to the couch and keep the windows open.

Mother's Day at church also required some negotiation with reality. I was able to sit through the church service, but not without adjustments that I feared annoyed the folks who sat in front of and behind me. I squirmed trying to stretch muscles that felt tight, and since our sanctuary was set up like a movie theater, with the seating area and aisles on a downhill slant, I leaned against my seat when it came time to stand and sing

After church we had lunch in a restaurant, which required more squirming. I looked forward to a time when I could sit for as long as I wished. It occurred to me we sat a lot for all kinds of things: education, worship, companionship, meals, entertainment. Lots and lots of sitting. Someday I would be able to do those normal things without feeling like I had ants in my pants. Just not quite yet. By the time we got home, I was tired but not taxed physically. That allowed me to go for a swim.

To many, pool time might sound like a nice, relaxed way to spend a Sunday. Whenever I swam, I was conscious of my limitations—maybe too aware. Memories of races and long workouts would come to mind. So while swimming six hundred yards might be a nice accomplishment, it did not compare with the six thousand to ten thousand yards per day I could swim when I was in my prime. Even at the height of my pain, before I had finally abandoned swimming completely, I could still knock out 1,650 yards, a mile. I only did it to soothe my mind. It kept me sane. Otherwise I was a head case. I wish I could say that it didn't hurt, but it did. But that was an increase in pain I was willing to accept to do something that really brought me joy. I just wish I had understood how to better manage it. If I had swum more often and shorter distances, I could have balanced things better. These were lessons that would have been far more helpful earlier in my journey. I am glad I learned them, no matter how late in the game. Throughout recovery I adjusted all types of expectations. When Mother's Day rolled around that year, I can't say that my goal was to swim six thousand yards in two hours. But three thousand sounded like a reasonable goal; that would be about what I needed to swim with the US Masters team. Tim's positive way of seeing things was influencing my negativity. Finally, I could see six hundred yards not as a failure but as an opportunity to eventually reach three thousand yards.

That meant some accomplishments made me cheer, but mostly only in private. If I'd told a roomful of friends that I'd stood for the first time on the flat side of an upside-down BOSU ball, they'd give me a blank stare. *Nice, Amy.* Yet the accomplishment, even though I was supported by balance bars, made me feel like a freakin' rock star. I didn't fall even though Tim had asked me to close my eyes and lose all visual orientation. These experiences made me feel like an athlete again.

Each step forward encouraged me to expect to be pain free. I listened to Tim and rejoiced as we continued to strip away the layers I was encased in. I was always wanting to rise to each new challenge, to make him proud of me, to be proud of myself.

As I started to feel more like an athlete, my attitude about the weight I'd gained changed. I felt ready to take on another goal. Self-imposed restrictions, fewer calories—I could accept that stuff as an aid to my weight-loss goal. Could the wish to lose weight and feel attractive be the reason I finally felt ready to restart a sexual relationship with Ben? I'd always loved sex, but resuming intimacy scared me. Ben felt the same way. And for good reason.

Before my surgery in Georgia, Ben and I had decided to try and have sex again because I was doing fairly well; the physical therapy had been making a difference. Unfortunately, the next day I had been a wreck, barely able to walk into my appointment with Tim. He had been stunned.

I had dragged myself onto the table and gingerly rolled over and onto my side. As he began kneading my butt muscles, I heard him say, "What did you do to yourself?"

I hadn't been able to answer.

"Aim, whatever you did, don't do it ever again—never ever!"

My face had been to the wall, purple with embarrassment. He hadn't been able to see my expression, but he had felt the rigidity in my body and noticed that I hadn't been breathing or talking. That was unusual for me.

"Amy...how *did* you get like this?"

I whispered, "I had sex with my husband."

His touch and tone of voice softened. Now it was his turn to be embarrassed. "Oh, Amy, I'm so sorry. I didn't realize...I didn't mean don't ever do that."

Then he went into a biomechanical diatribe about sexual positions and how they pertained to my problems.

"Were you on top or on the bottom?"

"On top."

"No, no, no. You can't be in that position."

Embarrassment had turned into anatomy and physiology lectures that took the sexy out of sex. I'd never heard anything like it. But afterward, he had offered helpful suggestions.

"Be on the bottom; support your lower back with a pillow. You'll be more comfortable, and there will be less stress. Here, let me get you a picture. No! That sounded really weird. There are resources; that's what I meant. I'll have them for you at your next appointment."

Tim had been reaching out well beyond his comfort zone to try to ease my suffering. The memory is sweet, especially when compared to talks with my ob-gyn, who would merely shrug when I mentioned sexual intercourse created pain.

The lingering memory of that terrible aftermath of having sex was like a cold shower—even after my surgery. On the rare occasions I could convince Ben to come to bed with me, we would plan it only on nights before a PT visit so that I could get treatment the next day, if needed.

One night, after finally making it back to our marital bed, I cried. Not out of pain but joy. We'd had sex. I had experienced an orgasm. But it hadn't hurt. I didn't fall apart the next day.

# Chapter 19

The little girls at the dance recital were so adorable I couldn't help but smile. Erin, my seven-year-old, was among the tap dancers who put on quite a show. One number was titled "Tutu Cute." Perfect.

When the three- and four-year-old ballerinas appeared clutching teddy bears, my heart melted. Most of them wobbled when trying to balance on one foot. One precious baby-faced child caught my eye as she struggled, and my perspective shifted. These cuties would grow up, and maybe one or two would become prima ballerinas with long legs and strong abs, but that would take time. On this day, nobody in the audience expected any more from them than what their bodies could do at this tender age. I was in the same boat: I too was growing.

More musings arrived when the adult ballet class came out to perform. I was envious. When I was dancing, I had always wanted to go on pointe; it had been on my bucket list to be on my toes by the age of thirty. That hadn't happened, although I had persisted until twenty-nine, even while pregnant with Erin.

As I watched the women twist and turn and stay on balance, I remembered all the classes I had taken in the spirit of keeping my core strong—Pilates, to tone the body, the abs, and butt; classes with lunges, the bridges, the clams; and the yoga, which had all increased my pain for days and days. As I looked back a decade, I realized I had conceptualized all the agonizing burning in my butt as being out of shape or having moved wrong again. It was honestly an exhausting internal narrative. Constantly tracking movements to discern what was increasing my pain had produced a pattern of constant vigilance. Every movement would be analyzed and cataloged into what I could do and what I couldn't do without the punishment of increased pain. All so I could follow the rules I had been given to manage my pain and tend my fragile body.

    I longed for the freedom of movement these women displayed. I was weary of constantly analyzing every activity and movement. I wanted to dance and be carefree, to move my body without fear. Most people would have noticed and thought, *Hey, something is wrong here.* Not me. I had gotten so used to ongoing pain that I felt like a complainer if I brought it up. I noted again that my beliefs drove my behaviors. All or nothing was the way I had lived for so long—overly aware and completely unaware, pushing through emotional and physical pain. It was occurring to me these choices might have been much of the reason for my suffering. My body needed a different kind of medicine, a different approach to heal. It would take more time to wrap my head around that.

    "Tutu Cute" ended with a standing ovation. Me. Standing. Clapping. A student of little girls who wisely were taking baby steps toward balance, grace, and beauty.

## REBELLIOUS HEART

I really am a rebel at heart. I try to be compliant, and then something in me clicks. I push back against conventional thinking so that I can carve out a different path for myself. Often I try to suppress my curious nature, but eventually it just comes out. As much as I had appreciated the dance recital and all that it had made me think about, I was in the pool one day when I suddenly felt held back and needing to rebel. Like a wild dolphin on a leash. As I swam toward the wall, I knew I was about to ignore the warnings and prohibitions I had been given by my hero, my rock, my PT. I was going to do a flip turn.

The mere thought of it made me happy. I wasn't afraid anymore. And I didn't want to be careful anymore. Tim and others would for months and even years to come advise me to be careful when swimming. But otherwise I was free to do whatever exercise I wanted. It stopped making sense that I should restrict myself in water. I didn't like how the cautious reminders reinforced a narrative of fragility.

Have you ever seen a dolphin grin ear to ear? That was me as I accelerated into the wall, spun my body around, and launched off from the tiled surface. As I darted toward the opposite end of the pool, I was on alert for anything physical that might not be right. But no red light began to blink. There was no siren or other warning signal. All systems were go, so I did it again—cautiously.

My nonconformity wasn't about being difficult or ornery. Those moments were like a ray of light piercing the clouds. They raised me up and out of the ordinary. Inside I felt victorious and fulfilled. Maybe no one else noticed my heart bouncing in leaps and bounds, but for me the turns were a sign that I was gaining confidence in my body and how I thought about it.

I will admit that in this instance it felt a little strange to defy a man I respected so much and who would continue to help restore Venus to her glory. Tim was sensitive and skilled in ways that I found rare. His insightful questions, comforting confidence, and gentle spirit nurtured me; they fueled my belief that I would be OK someday. He also challenged me physically in each session, and that got me literally back on my feet. So it felt like a conflict that I was so ready to disobey. I trusted him more than I trusted myself most days.

Even so, further down the road, it was apparent that in this phase I was rounding a corner and moving toward a whole new way of thinking about pain and wellness and what it meant to have one's life back. A spark of empowerment and being able to rely on myself appeared—a spark of trusting my own voice. It had been so long since I had listened to that voice. As much as I exercised my body, I would also need to exercise my ability to trust and rely on myself to be fully well. Little did I know at the time, these dissenting moments would one day lead me to an unexpected career, a return to competitive swimming, and a fresh purpose in life: to help other women who were suffering from similar pain see the light and learn to feel safe in their bodies.

My adventurousness did not go entirely unnoticed. After sharing my exploits to my Facebook friends, I received a note from Becky, the physical therapist who had prepared me for surgery. Once again, she cautioned me not to be too sure of myself too soon. But six months post-op hardly seemed too soon.

Nevertheless, I stayed away from the pool the next day and took a two-mile walk. It took thirty-six minutes, but it was a bright, sunny, eighty-two-degree day. It felt great to be outdoors. I grabbed my hubby's iPod, put on my sneakers, and just started walking. I was tired of being out of shape and squishy. I could feel my body coming back, and I wanted to see how hard I could push it. I wanted to stretch boundaries. I got about a mile and a half into the walk and noticed that my muscles were starting to feel stressed and tight. My stride was changing. I almost stopped but then remembered Tim telling me that the changes I felt were my body's way of dealing with these endless muscle imbalances and weaknesses I was battling. So with that explanation of muscles tight and weak, I sat down and stretched. Then my athlete's mentality took over. I turned up the iPod with a favorite tune ("Flood," by They Might Be Giants) and walked the rest of the way home with a slightly smaller stride.

By the time I got home, I could feel the muscles in my knee, thigh, and butt spasming and bouncing like popcorn. They didn't hurt, but they pulsed. I hung off the kitchen counter to stretch; I packed my hips and butt into ice and prepared an Epsom salt bath with some camphor and methanol. It smelled like an athletic training room. Safe, comforting, and exhilarating. I had set a physical goal and accomplished it! I had a plan to care for my body after it was over. It felt good. The music, the fresh air, the accomplishment, even the smells and sensations of my postwalk self-care. Maybe I was getting the hang of this recovery thing. It was nice to approach something with confidence instead of fear or trepidation for a change.

Three hours later, the spasms stopped, my low back was a dull ache, and my glutes complained, "What the heck!" Maybe I should have apologized for pushing my boundaries so far so fast. I just didn't want to wait anymore. I didn't want to feel broken anymore. I wanted to feel strong at all times. But the endorphins were still firing, and I felt elated. All I really wanted to do was buy my own iPod and do it again!

My defiant moments revealed a dark side: this constant cycle of boom and bust was brutal on my body and my mood. Sure, I felt like a rock star walking that far, and I had a momentary illusion of being normal. But ultimately the cost was too high. My next precious PT session was used to calm the flare-up rather than work harder to get stronger. The vicious cycle made me feel stuck.

It was OK to push limits and explore the new strength I was feeling. But that also meant I needed to be realistic and allow time for setbacks. Paradox was part of the restoration process: sometimes success is failure, and failure is success.

I also had to combat my sensitivity to people's impressions of my health. While socializing with friends, I got a lot of praise for restoring my body. They were happy I could join in with them again. Then one gal went too far.

"Yeah, it's great to see you walk upright and not have to walk like this anymore." She then demonstrated how I'd looked in past years. The way my body leaned, the limp, the shuffle, the small steps.

Despite the goodwill, watching someone mimic how I'd walked was hard for my soul to bear. It wasn't meant to be cruel, but it stung. The breath drained out of me as I got a full view of how the world had seen me for so long. My emotions went for another roller-coaster ride, and my pain seemed to increase. I paused to wonder why.

In my angry moments, I felt impatience with medical professionals who had seemed to need to justify their methods by burdening me with their explanations. Yes, they had been knowledgeable; they'd earned their credentials, even if most of them never had been able to help me progress. At times, I had felt verbally battered with phrases like "muscle imbalances" that were supposed to explain why my body could not properly function.

And yeah, finally I knew I was getting better, but meanwhile I was also baffled by the persistent pain. Was it all really in my head? The doctor convinces the patient why she's a wreck, and initially there is relief. *Ah, that's why I limp.* At the same time, it embeds a negative image that is hard to walk away from. Here again I felt the need to challenge conventional thinking.

I was on the brink of new discoveries that would continue to grow when I began to study-the science behind pain. These insightful pieces of information would bring me new ways to process my pain, and I would eventually use my own experience to test them. It would take time for me to gain a new understanding of my pain, but the journey would be worth it.

## SUMMER VACATION

It sounds so carefree. School lets out for the year, and children can run outside and play throughout the summer months. Parents, on the other hand, wonder how they will survive it all. Especially moms with pain.

I worked desperately with Tim so I could play the role of a pain-free mama doing a trillion things with her two energetic and amazing kids. In my case, I would have to lower expectations and keep an ice pack handy. I was not fearless, but I was in a better frame of mind and stronger physically. I knew I'd be sore and tight on some days, but that could be fixed.

During one of our therapy sessions, Tim looked at me while I was performing one of our new and harder exercises and said, "Hey, Aim, what are you going to do now that you can?"

I was shocked silent. His words bounced off the inside of my head—now that I *can*. I was capable; I was able; I had a future...

He said I could do anything I wanted to and asked what was next for me. Speaking? Write a book? Teach? Become a PT? A surgeon? As far as he was concerned, the sky was the limit; I could have whatever I put my mind to. I just needed to figure out what that was.

A new career in physical therapy would make use of all the information I'd devoured about the SI joint, pelvic instability, SIJD, muscle imbalances, modalities, and more. All the knowledge and experience I'd acquired because of my painful past would help build a new and healthy future.

My realm of possibilities had also broadened because I'd improved enough physically that the brain fog had lifted. I was having clearer thoughts about what life could be for me. This was important, given the years of having trouble deciding where to eat or what to wear because it had simply been that hard to make a choice.

As always, I was a sponge during my PT sessions. I asked a lot of questions, and thankfully Tim was a willing teacher. While I was doing exercises, he would quiz me on what muscles we were working and what they did. It felt like a pre-med course. I absorbed information fast and had begun to question the what, where, and why of each exercise.

Ironically, as my kids anticipated their last day of school, I was walking around with a big knot in my stomach because I too was on the verge of going back to school. The notion scared and excited me. It could open new doors, lead me to new vistas.

Was it crazy to contemplate school while on summer vacation? Was I dreaming too big? The bigger question was how would my intensely curious nature blend with the professional community? Pat answers, the type that didn't give you real reasons why something did or didn't work, felt like handcuffs. I wasn't going to be satisfied with pat answers because they weren't going to help me fulfill my real goal. My goal wasn't just a piece of paper—a diploma. I wanted to make a difference by treating women with the compassion and trust I believed they deserved from the medical community.

If that was true, why then didn't I consider becoming a physical therapist? Even the bold and passionate ones had their limits. Seven years of schooling, at my age and with familial responsibilities, was too burdensome. I just couldn't do it. But friends, family, and colleagues were all on board with my goal of becoming a physical therapist assistant.

As summer started, I opened the school application and began filling in the blanks.

# Chapter 15

By the Fourth of July, I was driving the car of my dreams—a convertible 2005 PT Cruiser. I had fought with myself before Ben and I had made the purchase. It was frivolous, impractical. A convertible in the Midwest? The decision had been made after I had convinced myself that the car was a symbol of hope and fun. Every time I could take down the top, I would feel free.

There was one more reason the car had won my heart. It was a stick shift. There was no way I could have handled a stick prior to my surgery.

The car led to another personal pleasure. Erin and I enjoyed a girls' night out. With the top down and the radio turned up, we went out for dinner, sweets, and an outdoor performance of *Seussical*, a musical based on Dr. Seuss stories. In the parking lot I tentatively pulled two chairs out of the car and walked into the theater. Every other time we had gone to this lovely little outdoor space, I had sprawled on a blanket in the grass. To everyone else it looked like I was relaxing, hanging out with my kids. But truth be told, I simply couldn't sit in the chair. As we approached the seating area, I was anxious. Everything changed in those moments. I got tunnel vision trying to plan, to predict.

What if the pain came back? The grass, the chair, the long period of time sitting for the play. I didn't want to disappoint Erin. I wanted to stay. But what if I couldn't drive my stick shift home?

All these thoughts took place in a split second. They consumed me until I had a plan. I could feel the stimulation of my fight or flight kick in. It was exhausting. I did not want to do this anymore. I reminded myself of victories, like walks into the grocery store from wherever I wished to park and the insanely complicated pony tricks Tim had me perform in therapy. I had this, I told myself. It was only a play. Before my surgery I never would have attempted it. Too many uncontrollable variables, too much opportunity for disappointment. Too risky. But on this night, I unfolded the camping chair, hugged Erin, and sat through the entire performance without pain.

During Independence Day weekend, I also finally got to increase my yardage and swam seven hundred yards without stopping. I was so at peace in the water and energized by my achievement.

Small revelations flowed throughout that July. I eagerly attended our local craft fair. Every year crafters set up their work in little white tents that lined the streets. Potters, painters, photographers, sculptures in every medium. I loved wandering through every tent and admiring the beautiful work. I secretly coveted the artists' skills. As I strolled with Ben and the kids, I was mindful that this was the first year in a long time I was certain I would not pay a hefty physical toll just trying to enjoy the day.

One woman delighted me with her work. She found used objects to create garden art. I paused at her tent and realized that the Venus was a found object. Pulled from rubble and ruins, she had been reassembled, polished, and then put on display in museums across the world. I wanted to approach the artist and say, "Here I am. Make something of me." But I just shared my smile and appreciation as we passed to the next tent.

July also made me thoughtful.

The six-month mark was, in a sense, my due date, a term every mother was familiar with. When I woke up from surgery feeling relieved, I hoped it might only take three months to feel normal. Then progress slowed, and I thought, well, maybe only five months. I was a bit melancholic, then I'd experience flashes of joy, frustration, sorrow, hesitancy, thankfulness, victory, confusion. Why?

Here I was at six months feeling like a pregnant woman who was overdue. She wanted her child in her arms so she could have her body back. In July, it was obvious that my baby—me, Venus—was not quite ready for her unveiling, there was still work to do. It was going to take longer. *OK, Aim. Carry on. And never lose sight of the fact that a gain is a gain hard won. Rejoice with every improvement.* I had begun rereading the pages of my journal to remind myself how far I had come. It struck me that God had asked the Israelites to build little reminders of him when amazing things happened. The thought struck me so hard that I began to keep my miracles or wins on slips of paper in a jar in the kitchen. It helped me remember how far I had come when I got stuck in my own swirling pools of doubt.

Tim knew where I was on the calendar of recovery. On my way out after a session in July, he popped his usual question, which for months had been my least favorite. "Got to ask. On a scale of one to ten, what's your pain?"

I thought about it, then replied, "I don't like your scale. Let's make it one to twenty."

"OK. What's your number?"

"On a scale of one to twenty, at any given moment... I'm usually in the one to three range."

He smiled one of those big full-moon smiles that reached his eyes. "Amy, that's great! That's fantastic. You know what, I truly believe the surgery worked."

This was a big deal for the man who had been so reluctant to fully endorse going under the knife, even though he had known physical therapy alone would not cure me.

The swim team my kids belong to hosted an end-of-season meet every year. Instead of medals, winners were given candy bars, and swimmers got to choose their race. It was lots of fun.

The final race was a parents' relay. In the three previous years, Ben, two former college teammates, and I had won the event. We would look forward every year to the friendly competition. Each swimmer would race one length of the pool as fast as possible. I was supposed to be wary of speed, but the thrill of competition—the adrenalin rush—would heat my blood, and the victory would make the painful physical aftermath acceptable, even welcome. Not only did I love winning, but it was a moment of an old life, a big loss momentarily reclaimed. The joy I got from participating outweighed any increase in my pain. In past years I had always asked permission from my PT, and this year Tim had said, "Absolutely—*not*." I was devastated. I had increased my yardage in the pool, and I was accomplishing amazing exercises at therapy. I was feeling stronger, more capable. Suddenly, I felt like I was being imprisoned for arbitrary reasons. What made it OK to swim before but not now? I couldn't help but ponder how crazy it was that one length of the pool could undo this much work. That little question made me want to test more limits, to see if I could do it anyway. But my restorer said to exercise caution. If this pain really was all about weak and imbalanced tissues, and that was the sole cause of my pain, I would not be able to hold myself back from busting out top speed for one length of the pool. It was beyond my comprehension how one twenty-five-yard sprint without a turn could worsen my condition or set me back in my recovery. This was the exact thing I wanted to be able to do.

I was disappointed that I would not be able to carry on the tradition and expand our winning streak.

But then something happened.

The swim meet was canceled due to rain. I was overjoyed. The decision meant our winning streak would not end. I could put my sights on the next summer, when I would be allowed to swim.

Keep moving forward. One day at a time. Keep your eyes on the prize.

# Chapter 16

By the time autumn arrived, I had decided to fulfill the prerequisites needed to apply for PTA school. Friends were still encouraging, and Ben had given me his thumbs-up support. I was actually going to take the first of many steps to become a physical therapist assistant.

I would help others overcome pain so they could live free.

Although I had visions of what my own life might become, I had no idea how things would turn out. Experience had taught me that the ride would probably be unpredictable. I'd learn more about myself, my friends, my family, and what it meant to love and depend on God. There would be growing pains, the need for patience, and the good, old-fashioned concept of just putting one foot in front of the other.

Yet when I looked at the coursework and saw that in my last semester I would have to do a research project, I thought, *Piece of cake*. I'd focus on my passion for helping people who are experiencing pain. That got me excited, even though that requirement was three years away.

Before I could submit my application, I needed to have observation hours at two different clinics. This might have seemed like an easy requirement, but it demanded that I stand for nine hours. That was even more daunting because I wouldn't be able to lie down if my pain increased.

Fortunately, as soon as the day began, I learned to accommodate my discomfort by changing my position. I'd sit on a stool when speaking to a patient and then stand up and demonstrate an exercise. At one point, I noticed a clinician lean against a hot-pack container, and so I did the same, and it provided comfort plus made me feel safe. By improvising I realized I could survive a full workday. That was a big deal for me. It meant that I was physically ready to take on a full-time job. That blew my mind. I didn't have to be the patient anymore; I could be the clinician.

Even so, throughout the day I took note of what might create complications.

First, treating more than one patient at a time seemed in conflict with my desire to give my undivided attention and care. As a patient, I hadn't like the jockeying expected of PTs, and I liked it even less as a future PTA. In some cases, the PT would be in the room but mentally was elsewhere. It seemed unfair to the patients. How were they supposed to give their best if the person helping wasn't even paying attention? I made a mental note that this situation was probably a little different at each clinic.

Tim had always commented on how easy it was for me to connect with others in the clinic and build rapport and alliances with them. He would say I seemed to understand and relate quickly in ways that put people at ease. This day in the clinic was no different, and it reminded me of my time with Young Life. Connection. Relationship. The importance of being heard. All these were important parts of healing; I knew that. Would I be able to manage it? Would the overlapping patients and tight schedules allow for these things that were so important? Would I leave work at work, or would I bring it home? The connection could be even more intense when working with people in various states of pain and dysfunction. I was proof of that. The sessions with Tim were not merely clinical; I needed emotional assurance too.

Maybe the bigger problem for me would be becoming too attached. My empathy would kick in; my need to protect and encourage and love the person in pain might overwhelm my home life. Balance was essential, or I could burn out fast.

My long day was painfully rewarded as soon as I got home. My pain increased, and climbing stairs was difficult. My butt hurt. But we still decided to go out for dinner. As we walked from the car to the restaurant, I grabbed Ben's arm for support.

The following week at my next appointment, Tim and I assessed my concerns and took action. We created a list of normal, routine tasks around the house that could be done without increasing my pain. We also designed an active lifestyle with flip turns at the pool and permission to take classes at the local gym, within reason. I hated hearing, as always, that there were still significant muscle deficits. When would they stop? It was an honest question. On the one hand, Tim was giving me enormous positive support and telling me I could do anything I wanted. On the other hand, he was still reinforcing the idea that I was fragile and physically weak in certain muscle groups. It confused me. I was excited about living a new life, yet several days after observing at the clinic I was still applying ice and heat. Ice on my backside; heat on my groin, which was so tight it felt like it might snap in two. It made me feel trapped in my body, even as I reached for new horizons.

My frustrations eased a bit after an awesome conversation with Christy, one of my fellow SIJD friends. She provided some perspective. We agreed that we were both in better shape than we had been five months before. Then she said, "But it's not enough."

There, someone besides me had said it. For ages I'd felt guilty or selfish for wanting more and wanting it faster.

"Right," I replied. "Even if I'm 55 percent better, should I be happy? I still wouldn't be living what we call a normal life. I'd still have limitations."

"Yeah, like big deal, we can now navigate a whole day in the house. I know, I know, that's a good thing, but it's been a long road to get there—"

"And we're still not there!"

"Darn right."

The solidarity was rewarding. There was a fire in me to learn more about this crazy joint and be able to treat others with this kind of pain. There was a need. I looked at all the women who were reading my Facebook posts. And though sometimes I freaked out thinking about the long road to earning my PTA license, I could not forget the hard reality of my first year of college: lying on classroom floors because I could not sit in a chair. I swore that this time I would not have to lay on my back to earn a degree.

Meanwhile, lots of ideas about my future were gestating in my brain. Maybe I could also speak in public and share my story with clinicians and their patients who were suffering.

Why not? My ambitions were in keeping with my athletic instincts. Mine was a comeback story. It was Tim who had helped me see it that way. He had reminded me of my heyday as a swimmer, before the events that had changed the course of my life so completely.

Fifteen years later, Janet Evans (one of my swimming heroes) was making a comeback at the age of thirty-nine. She was in the pool training so she could try out for the 2012 Olympic Games in London.

"That's a long time to be away from the pool," said Tim. "But now Janet feels ready to hop back in. Same for you, Aim. Going back to school, doing all the stuff you're doing…Hey, you might even compete again. You never know."

By then we knew that Janet had already set records during her comeback, and I couldn't wait to see how far she would go. In the moment with Tim, I let myself dream and smile inside. Imagining myself back in the pool competing against the gold medal winner—even if I came in last in a field of hundreds—psyched me up for my next steps. I was ready for my comeback.

# Chapter 17

My decision to become a PTA meant I was signing up for a long-term plan of three years: one year of prerequisites to get into the program (retaking a couple of classes because of how old I was), then applying for the actual PTA program and doing two years of that. Many people might not have seen that as an enormous ocean to swim, but I sure did, because I'd been underwater for so long with back pain. Through the years, I'd lost the habit, or courage, to plan that far ahead with confidence. All I had been able to do was survive one day—or one hour—at a time, with no expectations beyond a short interval. Pain is very inconvenient when it comes to planning. It consumes. Making this commitment to school meant I was more certain than not that pain wouldn't consume me and my newfound dream.

I hoped that committing to the classes would change the darker, moodier attitude that had moved in like a storm front. My irritations were sudden and could surface without warning. Sometimes my menstrual cycle would knock me out of whack. Other times, I'd suddenly feel pissy just because one little part of me—a tendon, a muscle—ached. I was stronger than I used to be but still not strong enough. Even after good days, I had the urge to scream at the universe, "I am tired of being in process!"

To alleviate the moodiness, I took to an outdoor pool and swam almost a mile. Then I lay in the sun while my kids swam. Before we called it a day, I whooshed down the waterslide with Erin. We both squealed. It felt a lot more constructive than screaming at the big, wide, empty universe.

Even more daring was my decision to return to Georgia and meet with Becky, the physical therapist who had prepared me for surgery. I wanted her validation of my physical progress because she claimed she was an expert. Also, she was teaching a continuing education class for physical therapists, who needed classroom hours every two years to renew their credentials. I believed attending the class and shadowing Becky for a day with her patients would deepen my knowledge of SIJ pain and enhance my PTA studies. Her offer to attend the class free of charge seemed generous until she asked for something in return.

"I'd like you to share your surgery success story with everybody in the class. Let them know how much pain you were in, and make sure to tell them you are not in any pain now," she instructed.

It was as if she hadn't heard me tell her I was still in pain or didn't remember the several calls Tim had made to her. It struck me as strange, maybe even dishonest. A simple request for some people, I was sure, even if they were fudging it a bit. They might not have minded stretching the truth and saying, "I feel so much better. Thanks very much."

But it was difficult for me to speak publicly about my struggles. I was keeping secrets. Even Tim, who had provided the safest, most nonjudgmental environment I ever could have hoped for, plus my friends and family, did not know the depth of my doubts and fears and frustrations. I couldn't bear to express them all because I believed everyone around me needed good news, not ongoing complaints. And Ben's correct observation that I didn't like feeling stuck emotionally hardly scratched the surface of just how trapped I was in my head. My inner voice was a scary, unhappy camper. It would constantly ask, *Why does it still hurt so bad!* Or accuse my surgeon and physical therapists: *You said it would be better by now, but it's not!*

Then a calmer voice would try to counter or soothe my fury, for the millionth time, by reviewing measurable improvements, some of which would be readily apparent when I arrived at the airport for my flight to Georgia.

My conflict with Becky's trade-off stemmed from my purpose: to bring this topic out of the dark ages and into the light. That conviction let me know I was starting the next big phase of my journey. Maybe only one foot in front of the other, baby steps, but forward movement nonetheless. Would I compromise my mission right out of the gate by giving false testimony to a surgery that six months later had left me with mixed feelings?

There was another curve in the road I could not have anticipated. My SIJD Facebook community had led to new friendships. One was with a woman, Christy, who had elected my same surgery and was also a physical therapist. We had had hours of conversations about the SIJ and pain and the research surrounding diagnostics leading to the label of SIJD, all in the effort to improve and clarify the process. Those conversations were rattling what seemed like such a clear path to diagnosis. Before my trip to Georgia, Christy shared a book that shook the foundation of my beliefs and understanding of pain.

*Explain Pain*, by David Butler and G. Lorimer Moseley, was revolutionary in its approach to the complexity of pain and therapeutic neuroscience education. Since its publication, it has become an invaluable resource for clinicians and pain sufferers alike who have found no relief from chronic pain. Using data from clinical trials and other sources, the authors made every attempt to answer the basic question I had been asking for years: Why do I hurt?

Yet, after a first reading, I hated the book.

The information was difficult to absorb, but mostly I just didn't want to understand it. I did not want it to be true. I did not want to believe there had been mountains of information about the nervous system and pain and a million other approaches to help me that were never shared or considered. I was simultaneously curious and furious. If I understood it correctly, the book was a newfound source of untold hope.

Then another kind of anger seized me as I pored through the research reports in the book. During my eighteen-year ordeal, why hadn't any physician, physical therapist, or other opinionated health care professional ever mentioned these findings? How could that have been? I now had a plethora of new information I didn't know how to process.

That was the conflicted emotional state I was in as I prepared for my trip to Georgia. I contacted Becky to ask about the research—some of it had been out for a decade or more—hoping she could shed some light. The research indicated things were not as simple or clear as Becky had made them out to be. I wondered how she would explain the vast quantity of information that disagreed with her methods. There were plenty of papers showing that testing for SIJD—the very tests I had endured—were not very good. When I spoke with Becky, she was dismissive of the information. "They're wrong," she said. "I've helped a lot of people."

This should have been comforting, but her response was not exactly an example of critical thinking. I'd spent a year researching the topic before I'd chosen my surgeon. I'd put my faith in that office and the procedure. To do so, I'd had to ignore or maybe even suppress a gut feeling, an inner tremor of disbelief. My body was telling me something was not quite right with all that I was being told, and yet nothing was necessarily wrong. At the time, I'd only wanted to believe that I could get well.

Now, on the eve of my flight, I wondered why my questions about the conflicting research and ideas within this book could not be refuted with facts, data, and clinical reports by Becky and others. The rebel in me needed to challenge conventional thought or anything else that didn't ring true. If I chose to work with a health professional, all I asked was that he or she respond to my challenges with strong, informed logic, not emotion. I confess that I could, and still can, get passionate and heated about my beliefs. Yet in fairness, I could also handle the pushback. Show me why I was wrong—with scientific proof. No one that calls themselves an expert should ignore reams of research just because it doesn't suit their narrative.

*Explain Pain* and my endless appetite for supporting research forced me to review my many visits with doctors and physical therapists. When examining me, no one had talked about my emotional state and how that might have impacted my pain. Some just dismissively said, "It's all in your head." If only they'd said, "Well, you know, Amy, pain doesn't *just* come from tissue."

Conventional biomechanical reasoning in medicine claimed that the things happening in my butt were the cause of my pain. But the authors and researchers of this book believed that while, yes, stuff was happening in my butt, that information was then traveling to my brain. This information then caused the brain to examine other file folders, so to speak, to analyze the whole being of Amy, including her history and beliefs. The actual pain didn't arrive until after that process. Therefore, the authors posited that I could help myself change my pain. This complex yet simple idea gave rise to the idea that I could help free myself from pain.

Little wonder that the book and my talk with Becky had made me anxious. When I mentioned my concerns about my trip to Georgia, some online friends and others echoed what Tim had been telling me: Your recovery is happening. Believe in yourself, girl. Look how hard you are working.

Anticipating flying also made my stomach churn because I had not boarded a plane alone for more than a decade. My memory bank told me it would be hard and possibly too much to handle. Midair flare-ups were my biggest worry. If that happened, Becky might take one look at me and say I was a mess. "You are doing everything wrong," I imagined her saying.

A silly panic, I knew, but Becky and I weren't meshing. Beyond the safety zone Tim had provided, what if a second professional opinion of my condition turned out to be negative? What if I was not doing as well as I hoped?

At the airport I had flashbacks about my previous trip, when Ben was with me. Images of going through security, sitting while waiting for the flight, trembling with fear and carrying lots of painkillers in my purse. At one point, I was surrounded by five women of varying ages who were in wheelchairs or needed walkers to be mobile. I saw the pain etched in one woman's face, and tears filled my eyes. It was like visiting a graveyard before your own burial. No! This was not OK. I didn't want to be like these other women. Were they going to Georgia too, for a visit with my surgeon? If so, would they ever get their lives back?

My head cleared when I felt the weight of my carry-on bag. Ben wasn't there to sling it over his shoulder, and that was fine because I could now bear the burden. Boarding the plane, I helped a nice elderly woman in a wheelchair put her bag in the overhead bin. I was not a massive train wreck. My life was better. *Your fears are irrational, Aim.*

That made me laugh. A little.

On the day I trailed Becky, we saw about six patients, all of whom were in pain. It was not for me to comment or instruct, so I watched and listened and was reminded of my mantra: *Just keep moving forward, Aim. Never stop learning as much as you can.*

Yet as the day wore on, the stories told by each patient had their impact on me. I couldn't help but compare what I was hearing to my own narrative, since I would be expected to tell my story the next day to the clinicians in the continuing education class. Before reading *Explain Pain*, I likely would have stood before the group and shared positive, encouraging thoughts about the benefits of the surgery. I had improved; that was a true and fair statement. But as I made the rounds with Becky, the foundation beneath my feet was shifting. I had begun to question parts of my previous beliefs to make room for something quite different.

Between patients, and out of earshot of others in the clinic, I asked questions of Becky. One patient requested that the body scans of his pelvis be analyzed. I wondered why Becky had declined.

"I don't need to look at the scans. I know everything I need to know."

Another patient was still experiencing a lot of pain after having had the surgery, and that too puzzled me. I asked the seminal question: "Why does she hurt?"

"She's not doing what I've told her to do. She's not trying. She wants to be in pain."

The responses to my questions had effectively kicked the pillars of my beliefs out from under me. I was teetering from too much, or too little, information. Who was right? By then I was certainly aware of the challenges alternative medicine—homeopathy, acupuncture, chiropractic, naturopathy, ancient Chinese remedies, etc.—had brought to traditional schools of thought. Now I was clinging to what I had been taught because I could not face the fringe notion that I'd been sold a false bill of goods. My surgery had not been necessary.

Why would I keep a death grip on what Becky and others had shared with me?

My pattern, up until then, had been to default to authority figures. I didn't trust myself to make my own significant decisions for one reason: Jeff, my Christian mentor, the man who had introduced me to the sensual life, the man I would later learn was an abuser of underage girls and who would be sent to prison for his crimes. How could I trust myself after that blunder?

The next day, these were the psychosocial pieces at play in my mind as I stood before the physical therapists who were eager to know how my surgery had gone.

Before my presentation, Becky had made clear that she hoped I would tell the clinicians that surgery was awesome, a 100 percent success, and I was doing really well. When I reminded her that I was still experiencing pain and might need another six months to reach the finish line, I was rebuked. "That's in your head. You just want to hurt. I fixed you."

My purpose in becoming a physical therapist assistant was to be the kind of person who was not hurting others. So my fifteen minutes of fame, standing before the class, ended with the truth: I was on the road to full recovery, and my thoughts about the process were evolving. I was frustrated that at this point I could not claim to be an icon of SIJD. I was not yet the Venus de Milo.

# Chapter 18

I knew I was moving into uncharted territory the day I pulled on my first pair of high heels since I was eighteen years old. I'd stayed away from the shoes because as a woman who stands five feet ten and has a history of SI problems, I figured I should be happy with nothing taller than a "kitten" heel.

But our weekend out of town inspired me to literally take new steps. After more than two hours in the car, we arrived at my parents' home, where we attended a family party from 1:00 to 7:00 p.m., then attended a play with dinner at a restaurant afterward. I did it all in high heels and didn't need meds, ice, or heat when the day was finally done. But fifteen minutes with my TENS unit helped loosen me up.

The progress was sweet because within a week school would start. Just two classes, but I needed them to go well if my application to the PTA program was to be accepted. My excitement was diluted by fears that my body would fail me again, just as I was committing to a grand new plan. It was a mental cycle. I'd been around this merry-go-round a lot, so I promised myself that I wouldn't let it capsize me.

Yet even friends reminded me that this next year would be very different from the previous. More would be coming at me—I would feel overwhelmed, at times—because I'd not been able to move and do much for so long. This would be the first year that I had signed up for big things.

As I prepared for school, I continued to work through the list of domestic tasks Tim had devised for me. I vacuumed my living room for the first time in close to a year, and transferring weight from one foot to the other went well. Not that it was quite as easy as those idealized 1950s advertisements of impeccable women doing chores. But I smiled as I worked and didn't need meds or an ice pack afterward. So I called it a victory!

Swimming remained the best part of my days and weeks. I didn't count yardage; I just let myself enjoy the feel of the water on my skin. I felt so normal when I was in the pool. Every week it got easier to move, and it was a thrill to finally be able to swim long enough to feel fatigue and burn off some calories. I'd started a seventeen-day diet that demanded I swear off ice cream and high-calorie Starbucks beverages. My waistline thinned as my wallet got thicker.

There was an encouraging development that came at the expense of Ben. He'd walked with me into the pool to treat the neuropathy symptoms he felt in his feet. Stabbing pains, tingling, and numbness were slowing him down, which was ironic because throughout our marriage he'd been Mr. Speedy and I'd never been able to keep up. On this day, he called out, "Hey, Aim, slow down—I can't keep up." We had to laugh.

Other discoveries kept coming. While cleaning up the family computer, I found a quote. Although I couldn't find the name of the writer, whoever wrote it was speaking for me: "Why do I swim? 'I swim for success, success in the ultimate contest, the contest of me against myself.'"

What was in control? Me or my body? Swimming was the answer. Every time I was in the water, I was in control, the master of my destiny. When I didn't swim, my body took over.

## FIRST DAY

The day finally came when my world would expand, and a new life would emerge.

My recovery would continue, but I could not allow my pain to stop me with the plea for ice, TENS, ultrasound, stretching, or massage on demand. Now that the training wheels were coming off, I had to act like a normal person. I would need to get through my day without succumbing to the endless assaults on perfection.

Emotion took over as I contemplated my first class on Monday, learning medical terminology. The anxiety gripped harder when I thought about Tuesdays and Thursdays, when I'd study anatomy and physiology.

Everything made me cry because the future I did not dare consider a year ago was now waiting for me beyond my doorstep. All I had to do was go out and get it.

The Sunday before it all began, I listened to my pastor deliver a sermon about change.

"God takes us from where we were to a new life. And He doesn't give explicit directions. He just says, 'Follow me.'"

I watched as new members lined up to be baptized in a huge full-immersion water tank in their Sunday best. I was in a different head space than those good people. I'd already committed my life to Christ almost twenty-two years before. And yet I remembered the feeling of rebirth. The joy as the old retreated and the new arrived. All those years ago I had accepted the opportunity to live life to its fullest, only to have some dimensions taken away from me. The baptisms urged me to commit again. *Today I will trust Christ,* I thought. The power of it made me cry for a long time. I fully understood that I was supposed to live in a new way. He had something in store for me. I would begin by taking faithful baby steps to wherever I was going.

Two days into school, and my head felt like it might explode. I had never had classes that relied so heavily on memorization. I'd never been very good at it when I was younger, and the possibility that this might be my downfall was troubling. I couldn't disappoint the people that believed in me. What if I tried my best but just couldn't get it done?

I was so distracted I couldn't concentrate during my PT session that week. In those times when I wanted to give up, I made the Venus de Milo my focus. Her image reminded me what we were trying to build. A body that worked right.

Still, I struggled with the new exercise Tim had introduced. I was expected to walk on the treadmill while resistance bands pulled against me. I could manage normal walking, but when he asked me to step with knees high, I could last only a minute. He had a tendency to vocalize what I was thinking or feeling in the tough moments. Sometimes that was helpful; sometimes not.

"Aim, we're just getting started." He smiled.

Often, I'd laugh and embrace what he was saying. This time his words deflated me. I wanted to shout, *Just getting started*? But I put a finger over my lips. Hush. Only positive statements today. As Tim began to speak again, I put my finger over his lips and shook my head. He got it and laughed.

Feeling fragile may have had more to do with my concern about school. I chose to push ahead and see how the rest of the week went: three days of class, including dissecting a rat; five loads of dirty dishes; five loads of laundry; 2,550 yards in the pool; driving my kids to and from a swimming clinic; cooking dinner.

But despite all those chores, I was not mad at my body that week. I was amazed. I'd iced and heated areas of my body at night and sometimes while I studied. Out of habit or necessity? I couldn't really say.

Also, while swimming, a woman and her daughter swam in the adjacent lane. Afterward, the mother complimented my stroke and asked how much distance I'd traveled. Then she invited me to join their swimming regime.

They both wanted to do a mile—only 350 yards more than I'd done—in under thirty minutes. I was thrilled. We created our own little team.

School and PT provided a routine I had craved for years, and the two activities were complementary. The mental stress of my classwork made physical therapy a respite from having to think so hard. Tim would tell me what to do, and I would gladly obey. While lying on the PT table, I would take note of my little successes. I couldn't have been this busy even a few months before.

Tuesdays were the hardest. Sitting from 8:00 a.m. to 2:00 p.m. during my two classes and driving in my car and then a PT appointment. My abductors and hip flexors took turns getting tight, often fighting for my attention during my fifteen-minute walk from class to my car. The tightness, though far less than what it had been, was annoying. I wanted to be done with it.

At the end of the long day, I would arrive at Tim's clinic taxed and pushing against my physical limits. We'd discuss how much I could still endure, maybe reducing an exercise from three sets of ten to two sets. Sometimes I'd start by saying, "I don't think these are going to be pretty." Then after observing me, he'd say, "You're right; they weren't."

I had other worries, and I liked that we could talk it over and strategize.

"Tim, maybe we should change the day we meet, when I'm not so broken down."

"Actually, it's good timing. It's a better use of our time if you're fatigued. That way, we can build from your weakest point."

Call it counterintuitive, but he was right: he was training me in my weakness in order to live bigger.

## PRETTY THINGS

As my life as a student progressed, I felt the urge to try on dresses and shoes that I'd ignored for years. I wanted to feel pretty and feminine. I was redefining my sense of self. I liked what I saw for the most part but was not prepared for the reaction from others. While sitting in class, I noticed a man staring at me and smiling. I smiled back because it was obvious we were the two second-career people in the room. We were much different from the eighteen- and nineteen-year-olds. My God those boys looked young. I was minding my own business after class when the man came over and started chatting with me. He tested a few innocent comments, such as, "You can't be old enough to be a second-career person." Ah, finally I understood. He was flirting. But I was wildly uncomfortable with the whole thing. Ben had always said that I was the last to know when a man was showing an interest in me.

I had to break the news to the OFG (overly friendly guy). "I'm thirty-seven, *married*, and have two kids. I'm old as dirt."

That didn't stop him. "Oh, wow. That's close to my age."

A few minutes later, I excused myself and headed home. During the drive, I was astounded that the guy had hit on me. *Me?* It had been so long since I'd felt worthy of a man's interest. Then I blushed with embarrassment and a little pride. The guy had complimented me, said I was pretty and in good shape. *If you only knew, buddy.* Until recently, my wardrobe had consisted of yoga pants, and my natural scent was smothered by ultrasound gels and Bengay ointment.

Still, it was flattering. I realized that I was progressing, rejoining society. I was now welcome to consider myself feminine, a woman with a full range of feelings and desires. I was not just a lump of human flesh in chronic pain. In other words, the comments from the OFG had awakened me to the realization that it was time to come out of my shell. In his own way, he had helped restore me. I promised myself I would continue to wear pretty dresses and paint my toenails and do whatever else pleased and helped me reconnect with healthy feminine impulses, including sex with my husband. In the bigger scheme of things, I realized that I truly had begun transitioning from patient to person.

## GRADUATION DAY

The discharge from physical therapy was bittersweet. The first time Tim had discharged me, before my surgery, he had confessed his plan had not been working. Now, after a year of hard work, insight, and lots of patience from both of us, it was a sign of enormous progress that we had to part ways.

I totally bought into the idea that graduation was never an ending but a gateway to new things. Like graduation cake and celebration.

My last appointment with Tim was scheduled later than usual because he had to do an evaluation for another patient. No big deal. There wasn't a lot we could do anyway because I was still experiencing a lot of tenderness in my groin. In truth, the pain made me fearful that I would not graduate after all.

As I waited, a physical therapist assistant engaged me.

"So are you better yet?"

I wasn't sure why a simple question that was meant to be friendly irked me so much, but it felt like a punch to the gut. Patterns. Learned behavior. I'd been on the defense for more than a decade. I would still need to learn how to lower my boxing gloves. Yet it gave me an opportunity to assess. OK, my groin was still a nuisance, but my body was so much better overall. I took a deep breath, smiled, and said, "Actually, I think I am better."

I hoped my answer would end the chat. But she went on, telling me that recoveries could be long and hard. "You've worked hard and should be proud."

Again, she meant well, but her brand of encouragement just wasn't hitting the sweet spot. To me, it still felt like a criticism, a pronouncement that by now I really should be done with all of this.

Tim rescued me with a sweet grin.

"How's Amy today?"

He led me to a table so that he could apply heat. It had been months since we'd needed this therapy. He just wanted me to relax while he finished with his evaluation of another patient.

Legs wrapped in heating pads, I contemplated what it would be like to walk out the door. It wasn't exactly my pain-free Disneyland ending of feminine perfection! We would do some soft tissue work to calm down the groin, not hard exercises that proved I was strong and ready for the world. We'd likely go over an at-home workout plan. We'd take stock, and Tim would remind me that I would never be alone. He'd always be there for me if I needed a checkup.

I began to feel peaceful. Yeah, I was mentally ready for this, capable of change. I sat quietly and listened to soft voices float through the space. I heard a woman complain of back pain that frustrated her. Other voices mumbled about one thing or another. Then another female caught my attention. She was full of gratitude for her newfound stability. I looked up as she passed my cubicle—and her image took my breath away.

She was dressed in ISU athletic sweats, and her hair was pulled back in a ponytail. She took me back to my injury in late October of 1992, when I had heard that snap. Lost, afraid, with no idea what my life would be like and if I would ever live normally again. Would I ever have children and a husband? Would I even be able to finish college? Would it be worth dreaming and hoping for better days? Yes, my life really did flash before me as she walked by. Or at least the previous nineteen years did. I saw myself: a young athlete, writhing in pain, her athletic career on pause as she fought to get healthy again.

Then I remembered the year was now 2011, and I was finally graduating.

I had no idea if this young lady had SI joint issues, but I overheard her say she was a gymnast and cheerleader, so it was certainly possible. I whispered, "You've walked into the right office, my dear."

Tim had succeeded. We had succeeded. The Venus de Milo was beautiful, strong, a work of art, even with all her imperfections.

When Tim returned, he saw the grin on my face. He paused, nodded. "Ready to tackle the world, Aim?"

# Part Three

Being heard and making sense of your story

is where healing lives.

# Chapter 19

The CrossFit gym was large, fully equipped, and packed with about fifty physical therapists and personal trainers. I'd flown to Edmonton, Alberta, Canada, to share at a two-day class called the Female Athlete. I was invited to tell my story by a man who at first had been an adversary but slowly had become a trusted colleague and friend.

Antony Lo had landed in my life like a bomb near the time I'd had my thoughts about the reasons for my pain expanded by the book *Explain Pain*. He had begun posting things that were in direct opposition to what I understood about SIJD in the Facebook group I'd been involved with. Most of the participants were like me, women who had suffered long ordeals with SI pain. By then I had said a lot about my surgery and its impact. Antony had poked at my narrative by declaring, "What if you are wrong? What if you didn't actually need surgery? What if there's another explanation?"

The questions he had posed, seasoned with bits of reason, had been questions that had nagged me throughout my injury and recovery. But his manner had been so confrontational. In a series of private messages, Antony and I had begun debating the effectiveness of his approach toward the people and beliefs in the group. I had felt his blunt style was ineffective even if his message had merit. He had begun to school me on the latest research and concepts that I had discovered in *Explain Pain*. He had cast doubt on my understanding of the diagnosis of SIJD that I had carried for the previous eighteen years.

All the information had been difficult to deal with because it had thrown me into a frenzy of doubt. I had felt like my foundation had been kicked out from under me, and I had been struggling with how to find balance. The ideas had been disruptive, as had been proven by the reaction of Becky, the PT in Georgia who had claimed her approach had fixed me and dozens of other women.

The truth is, part of my annoyance with Antony had been the same as my initial anger toward the authors of *Explain Pain*. He had seemed to be telling me that my pain was all in my head, just as so many physicians had concluded. It had pissed me off. I had begun searching for all the information I could find and devouring it to rebuild a foundation that would make sense. A turning point in our relationship began when Antony had clarified his position.

"No, Amy, your pain is not all in your head. But you're not fully understanding the role the brain and more plays in your pain. You're only thinking tissue and missing how the nervous system interacts with the brain. If you're only treating tissue, you're not addressing other factors—stress, food, lack of sleep, to name a few. Tissue is only part of the issue," he had explained.

This response had won me over. The pieces to the puzzle had all been there. Pain was more than damage; it was a response to threat. That idea alone had been a major shift in the way I saw my experience and would pave a new path forward.

Despite our rocky start, our friendship had grown rapidly because of Antony's desire to help patients move differently. His message of "do something different" would help me grow personally and professionally. It wasn't until later that I would realize he was teaching PTs and trainers across the globe.

He had also listened closely to my story and acknowledged that I'd made good points about how to speak to people in pain.

"There are too many men and women out there that are nearly hopeless. They can't see a way out of the pain. I'm tired of doctors and other health practitioners talking down to me. And so are they," I'd pointed out in one of my messages.

Some of his rough edges had begun to smooth. Just as I had evolved through our many online discussions, he too had been showing signs of growth. I had needed his knowledge and his belief in me. He had needed my insight into people experiencing pain.

"I want you to come to my class, Amy, and tell your story to therapists and trainers. They need to be aware of what you've learned through your tough experience," he'd said.

I had had to decline his multiple offers because by then I had been working full time as a PTA and taking care of my family. I hadn't had a free weekend.

It wouldn't be until years later, when my last employer and I had parted ways, that I would find myself with time on my hands. Shortly before our parting, my boss had remarked, "Amy, I think you should teach." The idea had begun to roll around in my head and had been starting to build momentum, but after parting ways, I had been despondent. This had not been the way things were supposed to go after all the hard work I'd put into passing my boards and becoming a responsible, compassionate, evidenced-based clinician.

"Antony, what am I going to do?"

"Come to one of my seminars and present."

"But—"

"Amy, we keep talking about how important each patient's story is. So tell yours. In public. To the people who are going to put their hands on bodies that hurt. Help them understand the person inside the pain. Your experience will bring nuance and life to the research. You put a face and heart on the research because you've lived it. Plus, it will give you some confidence that your story really does need to be heard; trust me. At the seminar, just tell us what that was like; be you; share your story."

Antony's the Female Athlete seminar met in a small town outside Edmonton in a CrossFit gym. My job was to get to know the participants and help them with questions during the lab times and breakout session, where they would apply the principles being presented. On the morning of the second day, I was introduced and moved to the front of the room. My moment had come.

After a full day interacting with these people in small groups and helping them to challenge their own thinking, as Antony was asking them to do, I felt very comfortable as I began to share my story.

"It was explained to me and I believed my pain was from instability," I began. "So logically an increase in my pain meant an increase in instability, right? So wouldn't the next logical conclusion, after endless years and endless attempts to stop the pain, be to stabilize the pelvis through surgery? Stop the instability; stop the pain. Are you starting to see the problem with these words and incomplete explanations for pain?"

If I had any doubts about the effectiveness of honest talk, they were quickly extinguished when I heard gasps from members of the audience. In some cases, they were heartbroken by my tale. Nobody took notes or fiddled with their smartphones. I had their full attention. The room was so quiet I might have thought that everyone had stopped breathing. When I finished my condensed story, I reluctantly handed the audience back to Antony. There was so much more I could have spoken about, but my time was up.

Then questions and comments from the audience started. Some wanted clarification about events in my story, while others commented, occasionally mentioning their own clinical experiences. Antony ended up guiding a thirty-five-minute impromptu discussion that proved my audience had not only been listening but that many members had been receptive to my short, oral memoir and were trying to make sense of it.

As I fielded some questions, I was struck, again, by the power of testimony. Research would take them only so far. A real story had struck a chord that reverberated throughout the rest of the day and beyond.

At the end of the session, I had many conversations with PTs who either thanked me for sharing or shared a clinical problem they'd experienced.

"Thanks for your honesty," one attendee told me.

Another offered, "If I hadn't been here today, I never would have considered the personal things about my patients that you revealed."

Other comments were equally as moving:

"I see my clients as individuals now."

"Thank you for helping me see how I can do things differently."

"I understand the importance of listening better."

The impact on me was huge. I loved connecting with professional people. The seminar suddenly felt like Young Life for clinicians. My focus on relationships, which I'd developed in the ministry, came to my aid. It was natural to speak to a group. It felt like home. I too was a professional. I had something to offer that helped others while empowering me to step into a new arena of activity and accomplishment. All my years of limping around, doubting myself, but eventually triumphing had provided a unique vantage point from which to speak to this crowd. I was no longer bedridden. Here, in an environment Antony had provided, I belonged.

## BACK TO SCHOOL

Although the reasons I was fired from my last PTA job were never fully articulated, I know that it stemmed, in part, from my more holistic understanding of patients in pain. That approach had conflicted with my employer's sometimes outdated practices. I had been frustrated at being so shackled in what I was allowed to do to help patients. In many ways I had been a good team player who had just wanted to obey the rules. It had been my job to carry out the goals and plans set out by the physical therapists—in thirty- to forty-five-minute sessions. But I had also wanted to listen to patients and help educate them about how their life stories impacted their pain. There hadn't been time enough to do both, so the therapy that was billable had tended to win out.

There had been times, however, when my unique perspective on pain had been recognized and utilized. Often, I had been given the cases others hadn't wanted because I had had more patience than most everyone else. It hadn't been rocket science to me. I had just listened to my patients to learn what was going on in their lives, because that stuff mattered. I had known there were no magic one-size-fits-all solutions for chronic pain. Each individual had needed something different. By being attentive, I could figure out what those needs were.

My first job had required me to call on my desire to be a team player. I had been a flexible employee. My bosses had placed me in a variety of settings—nursing homes, hospitals, and outpatient clinics. The latter had been my true calling and my favored setting. I had left that job because I had been looking for a clinic and a PT that believed, like I did, that people's stories matter in concert with physical therapy. Each time that I had changed jobs, it had been because I had thought I had found that combination in a PT. Had I been too impatient in my search for the perfect fit? Maybe. But once again, I had not been a twentysomething graduate who had her whole career ahead of her. I had been keen on getting to the heart of the matter. My mission, my purpose, had been clear as day.

Throughout my PTA work, when treating patients, I had kept seeing and hearing echoes of myself in them. For example, a patient had complained that she had been doing exercises, everything she had been told to do, yet still had not been getting better. Those moments had rung my bell. I understood the frustration after obediently following instructions—for months, if not years.

Also, by then I had learned the importance of variability, that you cannot keep doing the same exercises over and over and hoping the results will change. If it hurts, change it up; find the movement that feels good.

Again, part of this had come from Antony, who likely would have agreed with Albert Einstein's definition of insanity: "doing the same thing over and over while expecting a different result." That idea resonated with me because that's exactly what I'd done. For various reasons, I had resolutely followed the leader, even after years of setbacks. It had been Antony who had pointed out that I had not strayed far enough from convention in my early initiation to pain and recovery.

Finally, as a PTA I had also been sympathetic to the patients who had cried when they had said, "I've been to all the doctors, and they don't listen." That had been like preaching to the choir.

Even though I had not been a psychotherapist, not by a long shot, I had understood that everybody had needed to talk through his or her pain and beliefs. Patients had needed to feel that they'd been heard. If the patient appointments had not been long enough for me to make sense of each story, my new understanding of pain had meant I would often be saying, "I'm going to tell you you're not as broken as you think."

Perhaps my inherent frustration with the status quo had seeped into my work with the clinic that had decided I was not a good fit. Looking back, I have always asked divergent questions and desired to see things holistically; many of my classmates and instructors over the years have found me difficult. I've always seen it as curiosity and a deep desire to learn and understand. I have since found many others just like me. The dual impulses to be cooperative yet remain curious and get answers to my questions had colored my time in PTA school. After asking a probing question, my teachers would often cut me off by saying, "Amy, that's outside the scope of this class."

Indeed, those questions had been born of a desire to integrate the countless research papers, conversations, and books I had read prior to school. They were another layer of my sorting out my own pain story and rapidly seeing I would soon be answering the questions of people in pain. By the time I had begun PTA school, I had had plenty of practice asking tough questions and only accepting intelligent answers, not babble that was delivered by rote.

Frankly, my classmates had thought I was a little odd. They'd ask, "Why do you study so hard and ask all these weird questions?"

In fairness, most of these students had still been young, a few just out of high school and most in their early twenties. All they had wanted had been a passing grade so that someday they could get a job. I had reminded them that it wasn't enough just to earn a degree.

"On the other side, once you've graduated, there are all these men and women who need help. We don't treat textbooks; we treat people," I'd said. It had been my way of explaining that I had wanted to learn everything I could so that I could be the best PTA ever.

School had also been frustrating because it had demanded that we memorize tons of information. But that act alone would not teach critical thinking. And pat answers had annoyed me because it had seemed that the new research that so many others had shown me had not been finding its way into the curriculum. Learning outdated techniques and concepts had frustrated me. What the heck? It had shocked me that I was being taught things in school that had been proven ineffective or false and yet were presented as current and accurate. I had been seeing the larger issue. Clinicians hadn't know any better than patients had that there had been research available that had been way ahead of what we were being taught and tested on. How many other men and women would need to suffer for eighteen years before stumbling onto a solution for their pain? I would learn that it can take decades for new research to make it into training programs.

# Chapter 20

A requirement during the second semester of PTA school was to go into the field for clinicals. Clinicals meant working in a clinic under the direct supervision of a PT or PTA to observe as well as get some hands-on experience with patients. It was much like the student teaching I'd done many years before for my teaching degree. I couldn't wait to get started.

Little did I know that shortly a careless act would precipitate perhaps the most pivotal moment in my journey.

In class we were going over stretching techniques for hip muscles. I was on a therapy table working with a classmate, Kara, who was practicing a particular stretch. This was a great opportunity to teach my friend the value of listening to the patient and how to feel when the patient's body was guarding—essentially to understand when the client's body is resistant to the stretch for various possible reasons. I told her about the screws in my pelvis and my history of pain so that she would understand why there might be guarding and why it was important to go slowly. I wanted her to sense how my body was responding and what it was telling her. This information should alert her to ask questions and communicate with her patient. She did an excellent job, and I was so proud of her. I had a wonderful sense that by showing this PTA student a specific kind of sensitivity using my body and history, I'd be helping her future patients as well.

As we continued to talk, our instructor, for reasons I'm still not clear on, decided to show Kara how it was done. Without warning she grabbed my leg and with an abrupt and forceful motion, executed the same stretch Kara had done but with far different results. In an instant, I curled up in a ball of anger and tears on the treatment table. Not wanting to move, experiencing that flash of intense pain again, I was afraid of what had just happened. The pain, that familiar pain. So intense, so blinding. I panicked.

How ironic. I'd just taught my friend to be aware and sensitive to the patient, to ask questions about their history and to have a feel for the muscles she was working on. And then my instructor, who was supposed to be the professional, proved my point by ignoring all those things I had just taught.

Pain! Fear! Danger!

Although I was lying on a table in class, in my mind I was a swimmer writhing in pain on a pool deck eighteen years earlier.

No. Please. Not again. Don't send me back into a tunnel of pain.

"Oh, I'm sorry. Did that hurt?" was all I would get from her as an apology for her carelessness. With no future concern for what damage she may have done, she simply walked away.

Like my coach at ISU, this was another person of authority who, through carelessness and lack of concern, had caused me pain and then walked away.

My head roared as alarms of danger sounded off. A darkness reached out and threatened to pull me under, to drown me in all the old thoughts of fear, guilt, shame, and failure. I was afraid to move.

Eventually, I limped out of class with a broken heart and searing pain in my sacrum, rear end, and hip. It felt torn up, and it burned. Familiar feeling. All too familiar. After I got home, I tried to calm down by sleeping it off, hoping that the pain would subside. But when I woke up, the pain had intensified.

I called Tim. I needed a sane person to talk me off the ledge and tell me I was going to be OK. Yet this time, even Tim was shaken. "You don't think she bent the screws, do you?" he asked.

I'd never seen him upset. He was always the voice of reason, assuring me that painful episodes had not harmed what the surgery had accomplished.

Not only was he worried; he was angry. He was furious that a PT and educator could be so thoughtless and careless. I went into the clinic so that Tim could examine me. There was little he could do to assess me because practically all movement hurt. He diagnosed me with SI and external rotator strain.

I cried all the way home. How could an SI joint with screws in it be sprained? This didn't make sense.

I realized then that Tim wasn't going to be the one to reassure me or to fix this.

It was as if in that moment all the bits and pieces of learning I'd been acquiring over the last few years suddenly fit together. I knew what I needed to do.

My pain story had had many authors over the years, each one adding to the narrative that set up my nervous system to perpetuate pain. My Young Life leader, physical therapists, doctors, a swim coach, even my friends and family. They had all contributed in big and small ways to a belief that I was broken, and I had believed that was my story.

Now I knew differently. It was time that I took over the writing of my story.

I made a plan. My own plan. I didn't wait for the medical profession to tell me what to do.

First, I made an appointment with Dr. Hancock and explained I would like an X-ray taken to assure me that everything was as it should be and nothing was broken. Those images came back clean. Armed with that knowledge, I could move forward without fear that any damage had been done. Knowing that made a world of difference.

The next step was to mitigate pain as best as possible to let my body and nervous system calm down. So I grabbed a pair of crutches to take the weight off. Why suffer when I didn't need to? I could use some tools to make life easier for the short term.

I realized that this setback could affect my clinicals, so my next step was to meet with the program director at school to explain what had happened.

"You can't go to clinicals on crutches," she said.

"But it's not that I'm damaged. I just need to—"

She wouldn't budge. Julie did things by the book. If you can't stand, you can't do clinicals. It was very black-and-white for her.

"No, Amy, you'll have to postpone the clinicals. We'll hold your position for next year."

I wasn't about to stop school. No way! Having to postpone school would make me feel defeated, the same way I had felt when I'd had to sign away my swimming scholarship years before. Pain was once again threatening to take away something that was I potentially very good at doing.

This was *my* story now, and I was in charge. I had a plan, I knew what this pain was and more importantly what it wasn't, and I was going to move forward. This time things were going to be different.

"I can only allow you to do the clinicals if your doctor writes a note verifying that you are sufficiently healed to continue," the program director said.

*Aha! There's my way forward here*, I thought.

Dr. Hancock understood my dilemma and was willing to partner with me. "If someone had told me I couldn't do my residency all those years ago, there is no way I would have accepted it."

He was willing to write that note and to prescribe some steroids and anti-inflammatories so that I could get through each day.

For the next ten weeks, I met with Tim, whose healing hands made the pain slowly subside—again. By then, we'd worked together at intervals over multiple years. We'd developed an emotional connection that was valuable to us both. He was protective of Venus. He believed in her.

"It feels more like I'm treating a colleague than a patient," he said at one point. That made me proud.

Tim was my cheerleader—always had been—and this time I would need his guidance and encouragement but not his explanations. He had me doing all kinds of exercises. Our goal was no longer just to help me function so that I could do the laundry and other domestic chores. This time, it was more like we were training Amy the athlete. We were training for a career that would keep me on my feet, and I still had an unquenchable goal to swim and compete again.

Tim wanted to start slowly at first. I had to remind him that I was not a fragile thing that was going to break. I wanted to be pushed to do things I didn't think I was able to do before.

Variability of task is very important in therapy. Basically, if one movement task seems too daunting, try something different. I had found that I still had a fear of jumping.

"But, Amy, if you're going to compete again as a swimmer, you'll need to jump off the starting blocks at the beginning of a race."

To make it easy for me, Tim stretched a piece of Kinesio tape on the floor. "Jump over the tape."

Hmm, yeah. I couldn't do it. Even the idea of jumping was stirring up those pain responses. The nervous system was going into alarm mode.

"OK, no problem. We'll try that again another time." He smiled and moved on to something else.

At our next appointment he said, "Come outside. We're going to play a game."

Yay! I liked games.

He drew a hopscotch board on the ground and handed me a stone, and we played. Without thinking I hopped on one foot, then two feet and then one again. He had tricked me, or rather my brain. Under the guise of a different activity, I was able to jump—something I had vehemently balked at days before.

It was one of our best PT sessions ever. It gave me confidence that I could handle more than average activities. Over the next weeks, we rapidly built on that success. Soon Tim had me jumping onto boxes. I was amazed at my strength and ability to do things I hadn't done in years. My resilience continued to build in my body and heart.

Fortunately, my first rotation of clinicals required students to be in the field only twice a week, far less than our last semester of the program when we'd work on-site five days per week. Basically, a full-time job. Only having to go two days a week allowed me the time to build my confidence of being on my feet and working. Because of that gradual exposure to standing and working, I knew that when the time came to work five days a week, I'd be perfectly fine.

For the first two weeks of clinicals, I still used the crutches to make the rest of my life better by not having to support all my weight while working. Thank God. I had a full life: school, clinicals, studies, familial responsibilities. This was no time to slow down. I'd handle this painful bump in the road just by staying off my hip as much as possible.

Yet when that rotation ended, I still had nagging, angry pain in my right hip. Again I returned to Tim, who rubbed, mashed, and massaged my muscles in every possible way, to no avail.

"Amy, how about trying a steroid injection for the pain?" Tim suggested.

Ugh! I really don't like needles and didn't want to do it, but after much discussion I realized he was probably right.

My pain management physician was in Tim's building. He told me that he preferred we do an MRI, just to be sure there was not some other problem causing the pain. That didn't fit my plan.

"Poke me with a needle. If it doesn't work, I'll get an MRI."

"But, Amy, I don't do the injections much anymore because I don't find that they are effective."

I knew by then that my belief in the injection had as much or more do with its effectiveness than the shot itself.

He reluctantly agreed to inject me. But first, there was laughter. He'd discovered the Xs on my butt. I'd asked Tim to mark me so that there would be no doubt where the pain was.

"You weren't taking no for an answer, were you?" he said.

The steroid worked like magic. Or rather, it worked like I believed it would. The muscles loosened, and the pain eased. My whole being was able to relax again.

It was my plan and my choice. I was writing this story now.

Venus was restoring herself.

## Chapter 21

The clinicals evolved as I entered the second and final year of my PTA studies. The instructors all had their own preferences and personalities. I was fortunate to have advisers who quickly trusted me with the care of their patients. It was a big boost to my confidence.

The school tried to give us a taste of the various types of venues where we might be practicing physical therapy. So it came as no surprise when my first rotation was in a hospital, where I mostly helped men and women get out of bed, just as a physical therapist had helped me after my surgery in Georgia. I understood the importance of the work, even if it wasn't exactly where I wanted my full-time employment to be.

Although the hospital work didn't excite me, my time there brought me in contact with wonderful people. More importantly, every clinical experience I had gave me the opportunity to combine what I'd learned at school with the divergent models I'd pursued outside of college. For instance, we needed to really listen to patients' concerns and help them work through their fears. The power of that practice became abundantly clear when I met Dee.

Dee was dealing with sudden paralysis. During the Christmas holiday, she had experienced some back pain. She had sneezed and found herself unable to move her lower body. While I never found out exactly how those things had led to her paralysis, I'm sure there had had to be more going on since a sneeze is hardly dangerous.

Regardless, Dee struggled to cope with a strange new reality. I treated her twice a day, and every time I was with her, I did the most important thing I could do: I listened. As she approached discharge from the hospital, she was scared, much like I had been scared of my own discharge from Tim's encouragement and advice. She was concerned about how she would live her life without the support of the hospital staff. Despite her uncertainty, she was amazingly resilient. I'd cry after every visit, overcome by her will to live well.

One of Dee's coping techniques was her Dammit Doll. When she was overwhelmed by her new situation, she would beat up the doll, pull on its hair, or bang it against her tray table. It helped Dee express herself without harming relationships with the people around her. But she still had deep fears about what life after therapy was going to be like.

I saw how strong Dee was and how much progress she had made, but she had trouble seeing that in herself. I got that. I often couldn't see how far I had come in my own recovery.

Whenever I saw improvement in my life, a victory either in therapy or at home, I'd write it down and place the note in a jar. As the victories multiplied, I would dip my hand in and grab one whenever I was going through a tough moment. They reassured me that I was farther along than I realized. They were a testament to the good results I'd experienced and a reminder that recovery is not a straight line. There are ups and downs and zigzags.

I showed Dee all the wins she had racked up in the hospital and suggested she start recording her victories. Recovery is a long road, and we need to take time to remember that we have made progress, even if we aren't yet where we want to be.

I visited her room late on her last day. "Are you ready?" I asked.

"No," she said. "Everyone here just keeps telling me that I'll be fine."

How could anybody be ready without knowing quite what was needed to be ready? Dee had never been in this position before. She was going back home to live and function without the use of her legs.

"Amy, I'm scared."

Therapy had shown her how to do many of the tasks of daily living, but no one had talked to her about how to function without having nurses and therapists around her each day. Of course she was scared.

We talked about each situation she might encounter, and I asked her to come up with different ways she could manage them. She easily came up with solutions on her own. All I did was validate her fears and help her to recognize that she had the tools to still live a self-sufficient life.

Tim had done much the same for me when my discharge had been near. He had helped me think through what I would do in various situations so that I could come up with a plan. I shared that story with Dee to let her know she wasn't alone in feeling the way she did.

"Thank you, Amy, for all your help. But mostly, thank you for being real," she said.

Taking the time to actually listen to and validate her fears helped Dee through the next stage of her return to "normal."

Another realization occurred after I left Dee that night: I might never know how things worked out for her, or any of my other clients for that matter. My ultimate hope for my clients was that they would no longer need me, but that didn't mean I wouldn't miss them.

## PASSING THE BOARDS

When graduation day finally arrived in May, I was not done with my education. I still had to pass my board exam in order to be licensed as a PTA.

At the time, I didn't feel like I was studying enough. A few times, I met with my classmates for group study sessions, and though the camaraderie was supportive, I still felt underprepared. Part of the problem was this thing called life. The school year for my kids had ended, and the demands of motherhood and taxi driver had increased, not to mention the piles of towels a family of swimmers uses in summertime. All the usual demands were pulling at me, and yet I had a monster test looming that would determine my fate.

Regardless of how prepared I felt, when exam day arrived, I had no choice but to dive in. The format of multiple-choice questions kept me in line. Not that it was a breeze to check one answer. Each question challenged us to respond as though we were in a real clinical environment. Mere memorization wouldn't cut it. Those of us who took the test that summer all agreed that while in the middle of the ordeal we had no idea how we were doing.

It took a couple of weeks before I received my scores. The wait felt like forever. Not only had I passed, but I had done much better than I'd expected.

Thanks to positive feedback throughout my clinicals, I had a job waiting for me, which was no small feat considering how limited the employment market was in my region. The day had finally come when I could walk through the doors of a physical therapy clinic and continue my passion to help others in pain live more fully and confidently.

I already had a lifetime of experience behind me confirming my ability to communicate complex ideas to people and to help people in emotional or spiritual crisis make sense of their world—skills that would again come into play as I worked with people in pain. People in chronic pain often experience similar crises and question their own value. They wonder if life will ever get better, or they may ask, "Where is God?" Since pain is about more than just a body part's hurting, the spiritual questions shouldn't come as a surprise. But providing answers beyond physical therapy wasn't my job. Or was it?

The physical therapists I worked with wanted to do their best work and see their patients resume their healthy lives. Yet it was difficult not to see the whole process as an assembly line, or at least formulaic. We'd ask the patient to describe the pain, the physical therapist would create a plan for recovery, and then after hands-on massage therapy, we'd send the client home with a list of exercises. Most of the time, it didn't feel like I'd done enough.

Accepting those limitations meant I had to be creative in the thirty minutes I had with my patients. So while putting each person through his or her paces, I'd stay in conversational mode, asking questions and listening closely to the answers. This allowed me to conduct the motivational interviewing that was necessary to understand where each patient was coming from, even as we fulfilled the PT's plan of care.

For example, I worked with a woman whose severe back pain would not allow her to lift her grandchildren into her arms. I was searching for a motivating factor that would keep this woman on track with her exercises.

"What would it mean if you could pick up your grandkids again?"

She burst into tears. "My doctor said that I'll never be able to do that again."

What? That sounded crazy to me. Never ever? Well crap! I didn't mean to make her cry, but clearly I had found an emotional hot button here. How was I supposed to tell a woman who took her doctor's words as gospel that she should not be limited by such a comment? Words mean things to patients. They can help the patients see themselves as strong and resilient, or, as in this case, they can reinforce their story of pain and disability. This woman was in her early sixties. She had lots of good living ahead of her.

After apologizing for making her cry, I set about helping her to see things differently. Her improvement would not happen in thirty minutes. We began with simple tasks.

"Can you bend over and tie your shoe?" I asked.

Yes. She demonstrated and felt no pain.

I dropped a light object on the floor and asked if she could bend over and pick it up. Affirmative again.

At each session I'd ask more questions and keep her active. I knew she was fond of gardening, so I seized on the heavy lifting often involved in that hobby. "Do you ever have to carry bags of mulch or planting soil from your car to your garden area?"

"Oh yes."

"How heavy are those bags?"

"Oh, gosh, probably about twenty-five pounds."

"Yeah, that's a nice sack of stuff."

"It's good exercise."

"I agree. So how much do you think your grandchildren weigh?"

She froze. Her eyes popped wide open. I'd just thrown a grenade into her thinking. Suddenly, her belief that she'd never pick up her grandchildren again wasn't so absolute.

But that was only the start. Over the next six weeks, we did many activities that reinforced her ability to lift weight equal to that of her grandchildren. And by the end, she too was convinced she was strong and capable.

She threw her arms around me. "Oh, Amy, thank you!" After eight weeks, she was discharged pain free and could once again experience the joy of lifting her beloved heirs.

Not all my efforts to show people a different way to see their pain were wins.

Another patient suffered from mysterious back pain. Her scans were clean, so it ruled out the terror of discovering a tumor or some other disaster lurking in her body. But they did show some signs of arthritis and disc degeneration.

One of the most interesting discoveries in new research I'd read was that pathological conditions don't always coincide with pain, meaning that people without pain are often found to have something going on in their body that according to conventional medical thinking should be causing them pain. I thought sharing this information might be helpful to her perspective on what the scans showed.

"Research shows that there are a lot of people with similar symptoms walking around with these problems and living full lives." I went on to say that arthritis was a typical symptom of aging, yet we often treat it like it's pathological. Same with degenerating spinal discs. It was all part of the aging process. A lot of people have these same things happening and aren't experiencing any pain."

She trained cold eyes on me and asked, "So you're saying the pain is all in my head?"

*Aw, poop! That's not how I saw that going.* Information I had hoped would help her not feel like she was damaged and falling apart had been taken to mean I thought she was making up the pain. This ship was going down fast, so I started bailing water quickly. But to no avail.

Despite my best attempt to reassure her, once again those eyes drilled into me as she asked, "What exercise is next?" End of conversation.

She eventually warmed up a bit as we continued with her exercise plan and she experienced some relief from her pain. Like most lower back pain, hers would likely have resolved by the end of our eight weeks together, and in reality the specific exercises had little to do with her recovery. She arrived with arthritis and degenerative discs and left with those same problems. She wasn't enlightened by my fabulous wit or communication skills. In this case, time had healed her pain.

Why did that matter? I had not been able to expand her understanding of pain. Another therapist might shrug and say, "So what?"

But if we cannot evolve, the next time we're in pain, we reach for the same old solution. A panicked rush to a doctor's office and a request for pain medications. We need to move toward self-reliance. We can't just seek relief from damaged tissue. If we want our lives back, we must change our thinking and devise a plan that moves us upward, not sideways.

Every patient is different. They all have stories, biases, backgrounds, things going on in their lives that color how they view their body and their pain. I quickly realized that not everyone was going to respond well to the way I treated. What works for one patient may not work for the next. The process would always be a journey of unexpected reactions and results.

I made many mistakes along the way, and I'll continue to make them. The reason is simple: the causes of pain are complex. Navigating a story of pain is as much an art as it is a science.

If I had wanted easy, I could have just done the same five exercises for six to eight weeks and sent them home. But I knew too much at that point. I'd walked that road myself for too long to ignore the heartache I saw in people. Their stories mattered, and I couldn't help but to listen.

# Chapter 22

Jared and I had a history. He was like one of the little people in the Bible. He was the quiet bystander who doesn't think he is doing anything special but, in truth, is an important witness to significant events and a steady presence in a time of turmoil.

Tim and I had had a long clinician-patient relationship. He'd seen me at my worst. Yet he had never seen me work in a clinic.

Antony had been invaluable as a peer to bounce new ideas off, which in turn had ushered me into new realms of clinical thought. Yet he had never witnessed the depths of my despair.

Only Jared had seen my trauma and transformation. As a student who had fulfilled his clinicals with Tim, he had been there when I had been in my worst pain. As a licensed physical therapist, he had observed me as a student in my clinical rotation. After graduation I had been hired by the same company he worked for and was periodically assigned to his clinic, where he supervised some of my patient treatments. What I appreciated most about Jared was that he had known me as patient, student, and clinician and had always treated me with respect—first for my tenacity in recovery, then for my intelligence and curiosity as a student, and finally for the unique expertise I had gained from my journey.

Jared's manner as a PT was close to ideal. He was always humble and a team player. He was curious but not driven by ego or a God complex. He did not believe he had all the answers, nor did he care to be an authoritarian. He was a truly kind and competent clinician who instinctually valued collaboration. Even with me, a newbie in the profession with a storied past. His association with my history united us.

Because he had no great ego telling him he had to be the one to fix people, Jared would defer to me on some cases, telling the patient, "You need someone like Amy." The idea was to match the patient with the right therapist. Jared understood instinctively that the level of connection and trust between clinician and patient (referred to as therapeutic alliance) was a vital component to a patient's outcome. Although I was under direct supervision of a PT at all times, he spoke to me like I was his equal, his colleague. His level of trust in me, combined with his lack of hubris, made working at that clinic a joy. Oh, if only that were true everywhere.

Over the next three years I worked in various clinical settings and had the opportunity to work with lots of different people with varying issues and levels of pain. The longer I worked in this profession, the more I was convinced that a whole-person approach was the best avenue for people to reclaim their own lives from chronic pain. More than anything, they needed a coach. Someone to cheer them on and encourage them. My years as an athlete had given me a deep appreciation for what a coach brings to the game, and that's mostly the role I liked best in my work with patients.

After graduation I was employed by several different companies. In each situation I was looking for the right fit: working with a PT who understood the principles for treating pain that Antony and others had taught me; someone who would allow me greater latitude in how I carried out his or her plan of care. I didn't want to be the all-knowing medical professional. I wanted to be a cheerleader for people in pain. And while I never found that perfect fit, I did have my fair share of successful days with patients. Unfortunately, those kinds of moments were uncommon.

It was frustrating knowing there was more I could give, and yet every day meant I bumped up against the constraints of the clinical system. Following the standard playbook handed down to me by the PTs I worked for blocked me from providing some patients with what I sensed they needed: more handling, more coaching from someone with a thinking heart. There was a gap in the system that I believed I could fill with creative, admittedly unconventional, methods of care. And sometimes I had to apply my ideas in an unconventional way.

Gordon, whom I dubbed the Dancing Man, was ninety-nine years young when I met him. His vitality when compared to others at the home who were younger was astounding. My guy could still drive and volunteer at a pharmacy in a nearby hospital; he lived independently in an apartment on the campus of the retirement village, and he loved to twirl female members of the staff as he danced down the hallways.

But even this senior sensation had concerns. He loved to swing dance but had begun losing his balance when dancing with the ladies. Ironically, he passed all the balance tests, and this frustrated him because his medical team would not address his needs. They'd say, "You're fine for your age. Why be concerned?"

I'll tell you why. Dancing was his joy. The activity went to the deepest part of who he was. It spoke to the meaning of life. Without that joy, what good was living to be 100 or 105?

Thankfully, Gordon became one of my patients. I say thankfully because working with him was the highlight of my day. I knew what motivated him. Obviously, it was dancing! So after I had worked him through all the usual dog and pony tricks for balance, I asked him to dance with me in the hallway. He loved it! For him this wasn't therapy; this was living his dream. His joy and determination to continue dancing motivated him to do all the work physical therapy required of him. In therapy parlance, this is called "training to task." Members of the therapy department thought I was crazy for dancing with Gordon and encouraging him. The nurses and other staff thought it was amazing when Gordon regained his mojo. They appreciated the joy it gave him.

There was nothing so grand as seeing Dancing Man smile when he twirled and dipped the ladies. It brought pure joy to a place that was usually heavy with sadness. All I had done was give him what he needed—I'd restored his confidence to dance. My therapy method certainly wasn't taught in school, but it perfectly fit the plan to get Gordon mobile and confident in his balance again. If I had gone along with the standard attitude ("You're fine for your age"), he would have lost something of immense value to his life. And what impact do you think that would have had on a lively man of ninety-nine?

After I'd moved on from that job, I would occasionally visit Dancing Man. The trust he expressed continued to move me. He told me about the most sensitive parts of his history: the gruesome things he had witnessed when serving in the military and defending America; the survivor's guilt and other traumas that haunted him.

One night I arrived at the nursing home for another visit. I was stunned that he had passed away in recent days at the age of 101. Why cry for a long life so well-lived? But I did cry, all the way home. I missed my Dancing Man.

Obviously, finding a patient's internal motivators is hugely important. Equally important is rooting out those ideas that have caused a person to give up hope for anything better. Greta was a little over ninety years old and living independently when for the first time in her life she experienced excruciating back pain and jolts of pain down her legs to her feet. An MRI revealed degenerative disc disease and spinal stenosis. Again, these are common to find in most people as they age and don't necessarily coincide with pain. The PT then added SI problems to her growing list of ailments and told Greta she would likely be in pain for the rest of life. These words wrote what she believed was the last chapter of her life.

When she arrived in a wheelchair, this beautiful soul was completely despondent. After she explained what the doctor had predicted, I said, "Tell me your story. What does your diagnosis mean to you?"

Her lips quivered, and her voice was shaky. "It tells me I'm going to die."

Greta had never been in wheelchair before, nor had she ever used a cane. Yet here she was with a new set of wheels because the doctor had said the imaging results meant she shouldn't walk unassisted anymore.

We talked about the scary language that was often used when society talked about aging. Every term seemed to be a death certificate in disguise. Medical professionals assumed immobility was as common as gray hair.

Not so. We started with standing exercises and discussed her pelvis. As it turned out, her hips were shaped differently from each other. Perfect symmetry doesn't exist in the human body, and this asymmetry had been her normal her entire life. Why would it suddenly be affecting her? And yet the physical therapist had instructed me to correct the hips, something that didn't need to be corrected. It wasn't necessarily the PT's fault that she was undereducated. New research can take seventeen to twenty-five years to make its way into the practices of clinicians. And even longer to be approved in a teaching curriculum in schools. Unless PTs are keeping abreast of all the latest studies, which is hard to do, they are operating on information that is often several decades old.

It took eight weeks to help Greta recover her confidence and strength. Simple exercises, encouragement, and the exploration of her own beliefs eventually brought us to that day when I announced, "OK. Let's see how you do on a balance board."

To witness a ninety-two-year-old woman grin as she maintained her equilibrium on a wobbly board was a bit like seeing her defy gravity. Her accomplishment was transformational. Just because you're old doesn't mean you're ready for the grave.

Greta gushed, "I've never felt this strong in my entire life!"

This is not a Disney movie. She did not turn into a fairy princess nor find the fountain of youth. Greta still had pain sometimes. She would need to manage it through the coming years. But most important was her realization that the pain did not mean she was literally dying. She could live life on her terms rather than accept a wheelchair existence and the utterly inappropriate label of disabled.

## FLOURISHING FIREBRAND

What I knew to be true about pain, people, and the nervous system made working in the traditional physical therapy system difficult. My search for a like-minded PT and clinic, especially in my relatively small town, was coming up empty. After three and a half years, I had exhausted every possibility. I found myself disillusioned and disheartened.

All I knew at the time was that I was reaching for something that might take me beyond the conventions of what my PTA license allowed for. I was not a perfect person, and maybe I wasn't the world's best PTA. Surely, like every other human being here on earth, I had foibles and flaws, and maybe I laughed too loud or loved too deeply.

For several long days and nights, after I was let go from my job, I binged on *Grey's Anatomy*—the television show, not the seminal text book written by Henry Gray in the 1850s—and contemplated what I had achieved and what I might do with the rest of my professional life. My experiences with Dancing Man, Greta, and others only served to confirm my belief that I could make a difference in the lives of people experiencing chronic pain. But how? When I decided to enroll in school, Tim, Antony, and even my husband told me I wouldn't be satisfied just being a PTA. Part of me knew it as well, but at the time I couldn't imagine going to school for seven years to become a physical therapist and hope to be a part of my kids' lives.

This much I knew: I loved helping people. But I was only at my best and most joyous when I spent my days treating people from my strengths, not weaknesses. That conflict had been weighing me down since my first clinicals. I'd accepted the challenge and done my best to work within an established system that I respected but did not love. Therefore, I'd seek different situations that would motivate but not drain me. Who could survive constant heart and brain drain?

Thankfully, my self-assessment also reminded me that I enjoyed the support of family, friends, and new colleagues. I was much smarter about pain than I had been at the beginning of my journey. And I had a story, a story I wanted to share.

Ideas about starting my own business had been percolating for years as my restoration took hold. "What would my company look like? Over the years, thanks to the internet, I had collected a wide and varied network of medical and physical therapy professionals that I would talk with on a regular basis from all over the world. As a group, they had made me feel welcome. In so many words, they had said, "We need you. Keep talking. Keep sharing." They were the encouragement and inspiration I needed to keep looking for a way to make my calling into a career.

Antony and I had many conversations about how I could best use my gifts to help people. He suggested I become a personal trainer. That didn't hold any appeal to me. For a while I entertained the idea of starting my own therapy clinic. I even hired a lawyer to investigate the possibility and found out that it would involve a convoluted business structure. So in the end, I decided to forgo the complex in favor of something simpler.

I leaned on my love of people and conversation, story, and miraculous or even common outcomes. I nourished my burgeoning confidence with thoughts of autonomy without isolation. I would be enriched by my tribe if I kept contributing to our progress in finding remedies for pain.

Finally, I had come to a point in my life where I felt free and strong, physically and emotionally. There was nothing I could not do if I put my mind to it. Fulfill a need. It was that simple, really. And all my training and employment in the field had taught me what needs were still out there and relevant to my set of skills.

My postemployment brainstorming and time at home also made me confront some family issues. I was tired of missing my kids' swim meets because I was working odd hours at the office. Swimming and how it taught people to cope and succeed must remain a key part of my life. I would be there for Erin and Connor, and I would also push myself to compete again. I wanted more hours in the pool. I wanted to relish the glide and glory of communing with water.

I am, at heart, a teacher and a coach. I'm at my best when I'm working one-on-one or teaching to a group. And I work best when I don't have to conform to a broken and incomplete system. After all, I'd been helping people work through fallacies associated with their pain in chat groups and text messaging for years. I hadn't just helped patients in clinics. I'd also helped many people nationwide and in other countries. With a little research, I found a few other people on the internet doing similar things and making a go of it. So why not me? It was time for Venus to help others learn to restore themselves.

# Chapter 23

Then there was Rachel.

There is perhaps no other patient story I have that both parallels my journey through pain and highlights my development as a clinician as much as that of my friend Rachel.

She came to me for recovery from back surgery. She was assigned to my care because she was a swimmer. And she loved being a swimmer. So clearly I had an affinity for her from the beginning. Our common interests gave us a lot to build on.

"I was a swimmer too," I said, early on.

"Really?"

"Yeah, and I was injured in college."

Dumping my entire story on her was not necessary. I'd share just enough to create a bond so she would quickly grasp that I got it—I understood the hole she was in. Having that shared history created a quick trust, and Rachel soon let me in on her fears.

"The doctors told me…They said I might not be able to swim again. Ever."

So many thoughts and memories surged through my body and brain. I could hear in her voice the crushing disappointment that comes from being told that your dreams are now over. I remembered how similar words had added to the narrative of pain in my own life. For a moment I even felt a pain in my SI joint brought on by memory of that kind of sadness.

Cautiously, carefully, I said, "Rachel, I'm going to say something crazy now. What if your doctors are wrong, and they don't know it yet?"

Confusion swept through her at first and then was vanquished by a glitter of hope in her eyes. That was a powerful thing. Above all I wanted this girl to believe her dreams still had life. It was one of my favorite things to see a patient become receptive to new ideas, greater possibilities. Suddenly a new determination took root and changed the perspective.

Then I reversed course. It was essential to face both sides of any dream. "But, Rachel, what if you couldn't ever swim again?" I said.

"But it's all I've ever wanted."

"Your pain is not just a tissue problem because surgery would fix that. We're looking for the missing pieces of your story," I said, adding, "Any time a person's story includes phrases like 'years ago' or 'I'm still in agony,' there is more to the story."

The convergence of my story and hers made me cry, but not out of sadness exactly. Standing next to her, kneading her muscles, I realized I knew what she, and others, couldn't possibly know. Not yet, anyway. I knew that she'd been told a bunch of bullshit, but not because anyone had intended to harm her. These had been well-intentioned professionals who believed what they had been taught and who had not looked for any other reasons for the existence and persistence of pain.

Even Tim, after all the time we had spent together, didn't get it. In a passing conversation after I'd treated Rachel, I let him know I was swimming again and that I'd be competing in a meet. His words?

"Be careful diving off the block."

Really? There was nothing to be careful of. There was nothing in my SI joint that was going to fall apart. Everything had healed. I was strong. And yet his words showed that he thought I should be worried about my body's not being up to the task. For all the amazing help he had given me, he was still just blindly stumbling onto some of the right answers in therapy. He had not yet grasped that pain was not only about the tissue.

I knew from my own life that being in pain is lonely. It takes energy to go out to give the appearance that you're doing OK. You don't want to spoil anyone's fun; you don't want to be the focus of everyone's pity. And above all else, you know that you're going to pay the piper afterward for being social.

But for people who love their friends and being around people, isolation can do just as much damage. The key is to continue doing the things you love while managing how you do it.

"Your first homework assignment is to spend time with your friends."

Initially, she balked. "But where do I put my priority? Everything is so draining. What about my exercises? I don't have enough energy to do it all."

"Well, let's talk about how to make it less draining," I countered.

"I don't want them to see me this way," she said.

"But your friends just want to be with you. They don't care what you look like. Swimmers always look like drowned rats."

From so many years working with teens in Young Life, I was pretty sure there were some deeper insecurities keeping her from spending time with her friends.

"I don't look like everybody else when I'm feeling this way. I'm embarrassed," she confessed, after a few more probing questions.

Rachel felt vulnerable because her pain was going to be seen by her friends. I could relate because I was offended when a friend of mine had said I walked like a tin soldier. Getting her to admit her social fears wasn't psychology; it was a means to an end. She needed to stay engaged in her life and keep moving. Otherwise she would cause more suffering than necessary without decreasing her pain. What would be the point of that?

When she went back to school, she, like me so many years ago, had trouble sitting through classes.

At six weeks post-op, her tissue had healed, but she was still in pain. For a good student, just failing a class and not maintaining a 4.0 average can be traumatic.

At one session I asked, "How do you think sitting is injuring you? Can you think of any others reasons you may be in pain?"

My questions allowed Rachel to come to her own conclusions. Then, when she couldn't figure things out, I would fill in the blanks.

I'd been through this already in college, and by now I had many other ideas for how to help her get through classes. For example, the space pen I had used allowed me to write while on my back with the writing pad upside down. Staying involved in your own life means finding alternative ways to do all the things you'd normally do.

Sometimes the pain persists because we're trying to do the "correct" thing, like maintain proper posture. Unfortunately, somewhere along the line, someone had told Rachel that anything less than perfect posture would increase her pain. But even for healthy people, sitting up straight all day long is exhausting. Shift, change; the body is not meant to be in perfect posture all the time.

I gave Rachel permission to slouch, lean forward or back, or sit in any position that helped relieve tension.

"Stop trying to sit upright like a soldier. Slouching is not going to break you."

I loved the days Rachel came to the clinic. And when her condition began to improve, she talked about the future as if she believed her ordeal had an expiration date. That meant she was intellectually ready to move forward. This was the fun part for me. My patient could see that the mind-set shifts led to progress; she trusted the process and no longer saw herself as fragile. That was my job. To help her be resilient.

Our mutual love of swimming became an ally. When Rachel confessed that she feared that she would not be able to jump off the blocks at the beginning of a race, we mimicked that motion. I asked her to stand, lift her arms over her head in a streamline—the same position as when she dove into a pool—and hop. Her expectation of pain when starting from the block or pushing off the wall needed to be challenged.

"If you can do that while bearing weight, why couldn't you do that in the water, where your body is supported in the water?" Questions like these helped to break the negative expectations of an activity that she loved and wanted to get back to.

Rachel's recovery was her own. All she needed was a guide, a coach who could help her by giving her the tools and training she needed. My job wasn't to play the game for her or fix her. My job was simply to help her identify the weakness in her ability to do the things she wanted to do. And show her how strong and capable she really was. In the end she did what I had done; she restored herself. She was the one who had to believe it was possible, and she had to decide to put her trust in me.

In the beginning of my journey, I had relied on the biomechanical approach to medicine that had been given to me. Most any dictionary will offer this definition: "relating to the mechanical laws concerning the movement or structure of living organisms." My reliance on that way of thinking had not allowed me to advance and become self-sufficient.

Yet when I embraced the biopsychosocial viewpoint, I discovered a broader framework for interpreting the world. A dictionary provided this definition: "of, relating to, or concerned with the biological, psychological, and social aspects in contrast to the strictly biomedical aspects of disease."

When we as patients in chronic pain believe the usual narrative of our tissue being the sole reason for our pain, it can create a feeling of being fragile, breakable, and fearful of doing anything that might hurt that tissue more. It makes us dependent on the doctors and clinicians who say they can provide relief by releasing this or manipulating that. Our body becomes our enemy. A capricious master that can attack us at any time. But that's not really the case, is it?

I was able to guide Rachel in a few short months through the changes in perspective necessary to getting back to the life she loved because I had stumbled around for twenty years in my own journey and eventually found answers that worked.

I have cried for joy over Rachel's recovery many times. In her I see so much of myself. A broken swimmer believing that she would never again be able to do that which she was so gifted at and loved. A young girl with so many issues going on in her life priming her nervous system for persistent pain. A recovery from a back surgery that she pinned her hopes on to change her life.

But thankfully—oh, thank God—that's where our stories diverge. She won't have to suffer for two decades like I did. I'm so happy she won't have to look back on a life of pain when she's my age. I had endured years of unrelenting pain and often wondered why. By the time Rachel was well, I knew why. My journey had delivered helpful knowledge thanks to countless hours of reading research, talking with people online, and arguing against the conventional explanations I had been given for my own pain. Then add to that the hundreds of hours of therapy I had received, the credentials I had earned at school, and the learning I'd done while working in clinics. All of the above had made it possible for me to help this young woman in a way I wish someone had been able to help me twenty years before. How might my life have been different? Maybe I could have finished my career as a collegiate swimmer and realized all that untapped potential my coaches saw in me. While I still wonder sometimes what that life would have been like, I am content with the one I have and where it has brought me.

Rachel is living her best life now. Not burdened with pain. Not weighed down by the belief that her hopes and dreams of swimming are forever ended. She is now a sophomore in college, and she swims for a Division I team. That fact brings great joy to my heart.

And while my own dreams of swimming may have taken a long hiatus from that day in the pool so many years ago, they're not as dead as everyone told me they were.

I owe an immeasurable amount to the people that helped me get to where I am today.

But in the end, the only person who could restore me was me. It had to be an inside job.

# Epilogue

The events of my life that led me here ran through my head as I adjusted my goggles and pulled down my cap. Though I couldn't see them, I knew my husband and my kids were up in the stands ready to cheer me on.

The official blew his whistle, signaling us to step up on the blocks, and I felt that same old familiar feeling as adrenaline surged through me. The anticipation of the race; the thrill of competing again. It was twenty-six years since they had told me I would never again swim competitively. I'm pleased to report they were wrong. I am pain free at forty-four years old, competing in a US Masters swim meet.

"Swimmers, take your mark!" cried the official, and the loud sound of the starter tone rang out.

I exploded off the block. No pain, no fear—only excitement and joy to be back in the pool where I belonged.

A restored Venus, a work of art, diving back into life.

# Acknowledgments

Thank you, Jade and Ben of Tonic Books, for believing in me and this project and helping push us to the finish line. My mom always said I did better under pressure.

Thank you, Douglas Glenn Clark and Karen Lacy. Without you, this would still be a mess of ideas dancing in my head, keeping me up at night. Thank you for your endless help in pulling my story apart and spreading it out on the kitchen table to find the perfect pieces to share my journey of restoration.

Thank you, Maria Alcocke, for your keen eye on the cover design and for being one of my very first Instagram followers before we even knew each other.

Thank you, Robin Nordmeyer, for bringing out the essence of me in the cover photo. You are a master photographer, and I am humbled at your skill and grateful for our bond that has lasted all these years.

To all of my online friends and pain pals: You all gave me a reason to write. You inspired me to share more every time you said my words helped you feel a little less alone. This book would not exist without you and all your prompting. Thank you. It was worth it.

To every patient who has entrusted me with his or her care: Thank you for allowing me to work with you. You teach me, you push me to learn more, and you make me better. You each amaze and inspire me again and again.

To Antony Lo, Sarah Haag, Sandy Hilton, Bronnie Thompson, Mark Kargela, Tracy Sher and all the other clinicians and researchers with brilliant minds who have allowed me into their conversations to learn and grow: You told me I had a story that needed to be heard. I'm glad I listened. Thank you for bringing me home.

To my children, Connor and Erin, and Ben: Thank you for your patience and encouragement. You are my strength and my reason to push on. To say I love you simply isn't enough.

To Tim Highland: You have always believed in me and told me I could be anything I wanted, and you were almost right. You walked with me during a time when I was lost and alone; I will always be grateful for your friendship and care. Without you there would be no Venus; thanks for finding me and helping pull me out of the rubble.

To those of you still in pain: This book is for you. It seems dark under the rubble of loss and pain, but there is light. There are people who can help. You are not alone; there is hope. You are loved. May this story inspire you.

# Restoring Venus Resources

To learn more about a biopsychosocial approach to chronic pain, check out these resources:

WEBSITES

http://www.noigroup.com
https://healthskills.wordpress.com
http://www.greglehman.ca
https://www.modernpaincare.com
http://restoringvenus.com

PATIENT PERSPECTIVE

https://www.paintoolkit.org/about/pain-toolkit
http://www.mycuppajo.com

PODCASTS

*Restoring you*, with Amy Eicher
*Pain Science and Sensibility*, with Sandy Hilton and Cory Blickenstaff
*Pain Reframed*, with Dr. Timothy Flynn and Dr. Jeff Moore
*Healthy Wealthy and Smart*, with Karen Litzy, DPT
*Clinical Thinker Podcast*, with Ben Cormack; Jarod Hall, DPT; Mark Kargela, DPT

## BOOKS

*Explain Pain*, by David Butler and Lorimer Moseley
*Protectometer*, by David Butler and Lorimer Moseley
*Painful Yarns*, by Lorimer Moseley
*Why Do I Hurt?*, by Adriaan Louw
*Sticks and Stones*, by Jarod Hall, DPT, and Jim Heafner, DPT

# About the Author

Amy Eicher, BSED, MAR, PTA, speaker, and pain coach, combines her twenty-year-long journey through pain with her love of learning to help others use their own complex stories to recover from chronic pain. She is the host of Restoring You, a podcast that shares health success stories, and draws on her experience as an educator and youth ministry leader to provide dynamic public workshops for clinicians and their patients. Eicher is a graduate of Illinois State University in Normal, Illinois, where she lives with her two children. Visit her online at http://restoringvenus.com/ or on Facebook at https://www.facebook.com/RestoringVenus/.